J. C. Ryle
for today

MARK'S GOSPEL

Prepared and abridged by
RICHARD BROOKS

using the
English Standard Version
of the Bible

© Day One Publications 2022

ISBN 978-1-84625-723-0

British Library Cataloguing in Publication Data available

Published by Day One Publications
Ryelands Road, Leominster, HR6 8NZ
Telephone 01568 613 740
Toll Free 888 329 6630 (North America)
email—sales@dayone.co.uk
web site—www.dayone.co.uk

Cover photograph: David Ross

Printed by 4edge Limited

Introducing Ryle on Mark

The Lord regularly raises up striking Christian stalwarts of the faith, and has done in every generation. John Charles Ryle (1816–1900) was one of the noblest in his own day, and remains so even now in our present century. He does this chiefly through his writings, many of them derived from his preaching ministry. These are magnificent volumes, fitted for Christians of all ages and experience to read and benefit from. Many of them are still in print today, with robust and inviting titles such as *Practical Religion*, *Old Paths*, *The Upper Room* and *Knots Untied*. Perhaps the most treasured of them all is *Holiness*.

Over a period of years, he also wrote what he entitled *Expository Thoughts on the Gospels*. These cover each of the four Gospels, and it is his volume on Mark which it is my joy to commend to you now. It has been somewhat abridged here, along with a gentle updating of some of the language, and using the English Standard Version of the Bible.

Ryle had some particular intentions in preparing these volumes. In his preface to the Mark exposition he writes the following words: 'But I can honestly say, that my chief desire, if I know anything of my own heart, in this and all my writings, is to lead my readers to Christ and faith in him, to repentance and holiness, to the Bible and to prayer.' He wished very much that these treatments of the Gospels would prove a blessing for both personal Bible reading and family worship. All this is very much my own desire in preparing this fresh edition, with the hope that it would be of especial help and encouragement to newer and younger Christians.

So, then, in the company of the man once described by someone who knew him as 'that man of granite, with the heart of a child', let us proceed together, in the light of the very opening words of Mark's Gospel: 'The beginning of the gospel of Jesus Christ, the Son of God.'

Richard Brooks

Chapter 1

1:1–8

The Gospel of Mark is in some respects unlike the other three Gospels. It tells us nothing about the birth and early life of our Lord Jesus Christ. It contains comparatively few of his sayings and discourses. Of all the four inspired histories of our Lord's earthly ministry, this is by far the shortest. But we must not allow this to make us undervalue Mark's Gospel. It is full of precious facts about Jesus. It is rich in its account of his works. It contains historical details not recorded in the other Gospels. Like all the rest of Scripture, every word of Mark 'is breathed out by God and profitable' (2 Timothy 3:16).

Observe first of all, *what a full declaration we have of the dignity of our Lord Jesus Christ's person*. The opening sentence speaks of him as 'the Son of God'. These words are nothing less than an assertion of his deity—that he was himself very God and 'equal with God' (John 5:18).

There is a beautiful fitness about placing this truth at the very beginning of a Gospel, for the divinity of Christ is the fortress of Christianity. Here lies the infinite value of the satisfaction he made upon the cross and the particular merit of his atoning death for sinners. That death was not the death of a mere man like ourselves, but of one 'who is God over all, blessed for ever' (Romans 9:5). Clinging to this doctrine, believers stand upon a rock; without it, they have nothing solid beneath their feet. Our hearts are weak and our sins are many. We need a Redeemer who is able to save completely and deliver from the wrath to come, and we have such a Redeemer in Jesus Christ, the 'Mighty God' (Isaiah 9:6).

The second thing to notice is, *how the beginning of the gospel was a fulfilment of Scripture*. John the Baptist began his ministry 'As it is written in Isaiah the prophet'. There was nothing unforeseen in Jesus' coming into the world. It was predicted in the very beginning of Genesis

(Genesis 3:15), and all the way through the Old Testament the same event is foretold with constantly increasing clarity. Jesus' birth, character, life, death, resurrection and forerunner were all prophesied long before he came. Everything was worked out just 'as it was written'. So we should always read the Old Testament with a desire to find out something about Jesus, for of those Scriptures Jesus himself declared, 'it is they that bear witness about me' (John 5:39).

Thirdly, *how great were the effects which John's ministry produced for a time on the Jewish nation.* We are told that 'all the country of Judea and Jerusalem were going out to him and were being baptised by him in the river Jordan'. The fact recorded here is one that is much overlooked. We are apt to lose sight of him who went before the face of our Lord, and to see nothing but our Lord himself. We forget the morning star in the full blaze of the sun. And yet it is clear that John's preaching arrested the attention of the Jewish people and created an excitement all over Palestine. It aroused the nation from its slumbers and prepared it for the ministry of Jesus when he appeared. Jesus himself says of John, 'He was a burning and shining lamp, and you were willing to rejoice for a while in his light' (John 5:35).

Finally, *what clear doctrine characterised John's preaching.* He exalted Christ, saying, 'After me comes he who is mightier than I.' And he spoke plainly of the Holy Spirit, saying, 'he will baptise you with the Holy Spirit'. More important truths than these are not to be found in Christianity. The principal work of every faithful minister of the gospel is to set the Lord Jesus fully before the people, showing his fullness and power to save; and then to set out the work of the Holy Spirit and the need to be born again.

So, then: how much do we know by practical experience of the truths which John preached? What do we think of Christ? Have we felt our need of him and fled to him for peace? Is he king over our hearts and all things to our souls? And what do we think of the Holy Spirit? Has he worked in our hearts to renew and change them? Has he made us 'partakers of the divine nature' (2 Peter 1:4)? Life or death depend upon our answer to these questions.

1:9–20

This passage provides a striking instance of Mark's brevity of style. Jesus' baptism and temptation, the commencement of his preaching, and the calling of his first disciples, are all recorded in twelve verses.

Notice first, *the voice from heaven which was heard at Jesus' baptism*. 'And a voice came from heaven, "You are my beloved Son; with you I am well pleased."' That was the voice of God the Father, declaring the wonderful love which has existed between the Father and the Son from all eternity. 'The Father loves the Son and has given all things into his hand' (John 3:35). The Father's words at Jesus' baptism proclaimed his full approval of Jesus' mission to seek and save lost sinners, and announced his complete acceptance of the Son as the Mediator, Substitute and Surety of the new covenant. What a rich mine of comfort lies in this for all who belong to Christ, for the Father has 'blessed us in the Beloved' (Ephesians 1:6).

Secondly, see here *the nature of Christ's preaching*. We read that he came saying, 'repent and believe in the gospel'. Repentance and faith were the foundation stones of Christ's ministry, and must always be the main subjects of every faithful minister's instruction. When he left them for the last time, the apostle Paul told the elders in Ephesus that the substance of his ministry among them had been 'repentance toward God' and 'faith in our Lord Jesus Christ' (Acts 20:21). In this, he followed the pattern set down for him by the great Head of the church.

What do we know of this repentance and faith? Have we felt our sins and forsaken them? Have we laid hold on Christ and believed? We may reach heaven without learning, riches or health, but we shall never do so if we die impenitent and unbelieving. A new heart and a lively faith are absolutely needful to salvation. Once penitent, we all need daily stirring up to deeper repentance. Once believing, we all need constant exhortation to increased faith.

Thirdly, learn *the occupation of those who were first called to be Christ's disciples*. Jesus called Simon and Andrew when they were 'casting a net into the sea, for they were fishermen'; and James and John while they 'were in their boat mending the nets'. It is clear that these first followers of Jesus were not among the great, rich or powerful of the world. But the kingdom of Christ is not dependent upon such. His cause advances in the world, 'Not by might, nor by power, but by my Spirit, says the LORD of hosts' (Zechariah 4:6). The church which began with a few fishermen, and yet spread over half the world, must have been founded by God.

Finally, note *the office to which our Lord called his first disciples.* He said to them, 'Follow me, and I will make you become fishers of men.' They were to become fishers for souls—to labour to draw men 'from darkness to light and from the power of Satan to God' (Acts 26:18). They were to strive to bring people into the net of Christ's church, that so they might be saved alive and not perish everlastingly.

1:21–34

These verses begin the long list of miracles which Mark's Gospel contains. They record how Jesus cast out an unclean spirit in Capernaum and healed Peter's mother-in-law of a fever.

Learn firstly, *the uselessness of a mere intellectual knowledge of religion.* The unclean spirit in the man in Capernaum cried out to Jesus, 'I know who you are—the Holy One of God.' Yet that knowledge was not saving knowledge.

The mere belief of the facts and doctrines of Christianity will never save our souls. Such belief is no better than the belief of devils. They all believe and know that Jesus is the Christ. They believe that he will one day judge the world and cast them down to endless torment in hell. So let us take heed that our faith be a faith of the heart as well as of the head, and that our knowledge has a sanctifying influence on our affections and our lives. Let us not only know Christ but love him and rejoice in him. It is one thing to say, 'Christ is a Saviour', but quite another to say, 'He is my Saviour and my Lord'. The devil can say the first, but only the true Christian can say the second.

Secondly, see *to what remedy a Christian ought to resort first, in time of trouble.* Follow the example of the friends of Simon's wife's mother. We learn that when she 'lay ill with a fever', 'immediately they told him [Jesus] about her'. There is no remedy like this. Whatever help from doctors, lawyers or friends might be sought, the first thing to be done is to cry to the Lord Jesus Christ for help. No one else is so compassionate or so willing to relieve. 'Cast your burden on the LORD, and he will sustain you' (Psalm 55:22); 'in everything by prayer and supplication with thanksgiving let your requests be made known to God' (Philippians 4:6).

In the third place, learn *what a complete and perfect cure the Lord Jesus makes, when he heals*. Jesus 'came and took her by the hand and lifted her up, and the fever left her. And she began to serve them'. The woman was not only made well in a moment, but in the same moment was made strong and able to work.

We can see in this case a lively picture of Christ's dealing with sin-sick souls. He not only gives mercy and forgiveness, but gives renewing grace as well. The sinner not only has his sins dealt with, but is supplied with a new heart and a right spirit, and enabled so to live as to please God. And there is comfort for those either who feel a desire to serve Christ but at present are afraid to begin, or for those who are already serving him and yet are cast down by a sense of their own infirmity. Jesus is an almighty Saviour, who never forsakes those who commit themselves to him. The pardoned soul is always enabled to serve Christ, and difficulties we now fear will vanish out of our path. The same gracious hand which first touched and healed will uphold, strengthen and lead to the end. The healed soul shall always go on serving the Lord. Grace will always lead to glory.

1:35–39

We see a fact and a saying in these verses which deserve close attention.

The fact is this: *an example of our Lord Jesus Christ's habits of private prayer*. We are told that, 'rising very early in the morning, while it was still dark, he departed and went out to a desolate place, and there he prayed'. The same thing is often recorded of him in the gospel history. He was praying at his baptism and at his transfiguration. Before he chose the twelve apostles 'he went out on the mountain to pray, and all night he continued in prayer to God' (Luke 6:12). In the garden of Gethsemane, he prayed. Though sinless, he set us an example of diligent communion with his Father in prayer. His Godhead did not render him independent of the use of all means as a man.

We ought to see in all this the immense importance of private devotion. If he who was 'holy, innocent, separated from sinners, and exalted above the heavens' (Hebrews 7:26) prayed continually, how much more ought we who are compassed with infirmity? If he found it needful to offer 'up prayers and supplications, with loud cries and tears' (Hebrews 5:7), how much more necessary is it for us, who in many things offend daily? A praying Master like Jesus can have no prayerless servants. To be prayerless is to be Christless. It will always be found that when prayers are few, grace, strength, peace and hope are small. We would do well to watch our habits of prayer with a holy watchfulness. Here is the pulse of our Christianity, the true test of our state before God. Let us walk in the steps of our blessed Master in prayer, as well as in every other respect.

The saying is this: *a remarkable saying of our Lord as to the purpose for which he came into the world.* He said to his disciples, 'Let us go on to the next towns, that I may preach there also, for that is why I came out.'

The meaning of these words is unmistakable. Jesus declares that he came on earth to be a preacher and teacher. He came to fulfil the prophetical office, to be the prophet like Moses (Deuteronomy 18:15), foretold so long before. He left the glory which he had from all eternity with the Father, to do the work of an evangelist. He came to show to mankind the way of peace with God, 'to bring good news to the poor', 'to bind up the brokenhearted, to proclaim liberty to the captives, and the opening of the prison to those who are bound' (Isaiah 61:1), to bring pardon to the chief of sinners.

We ought to observe here what honour the Lord Jesus puts on the office of preacher. It is one which he, the eternal Son of God, undertook. By preaching, the church of Christ was first gathered together and founded, and by preaching it has ever been maintained in health and prosperity. By preaching, sinners are awakened, enquirers are led on, saints are built up, and the gospel is carried to the heathen world. It is God's grand ordinance for converting and saving souls. The faithful preacher of the gospel is handling the very weapon which the Son of God was not ashamed to employ.

1:40–45

These verses record how Jesus healed a leper. Of all his miracles of healing, none probably were more marvellous than those performed on people with leprosy.

Realise first of all, *the dreadful nature of the disease which Jesus cured.* In Bible lands it was not uncommon. It was no mere skin problem, but a radical disease of the entire person. It attacked not only the skin, but the blood, flesh and bones as well. Moreover, among the Jews the leper was regarded as being unclean and was cut off from the congregation of Israel and all religious ceremonies. Such a sufferer had to live in a separate house, with no one being allowed to touch him or minister to him.

Yet this disease speaks of something more: the plague of sin. Sin is a foul disease which is ingrained in our very nature and clings to us with a deadly force. Like leprosy, sin is a deep-seated disease infecting every part of our nature—heart, will, conscience, understanding, memory and affections. Like leprosy, sin makes us loathsome and abominable, unfit both for the company of God and the glory of heaven. Worst of all, it is a disease from which no person is exempt, for, in God's sight, 'We have all become like one who is unclean' (Isaiah 64:6).

Do we know these things for ourselves? Have we discovered our own sinfulness, guilt and corruption? To know our disease is one step towards a cure. It is the misery and ruin of many souls that they never yet saw their sins and their need.

Learn secondly, *the wondrous and almighty power of the Lord Jesus Christ.* We are told that the unhappy leper 'came to him, imploring him, and kneeling said to him, "If you will, you can make me clean."' And what happened? 'Moved with pity, he [Jesus] stretched out his hand and touched him and said to him, "I will; be clean."' At once the cure was effected and the man was healed. It was but a word and a touch, and there stands before the Lord—not a leper, but a sound and healthy man.

Surely the change must have been like life from the dead for this man. In the morning he was a miserable being, more dead than alive, his very existence a burden. In the evening he was full of hope and joy, and able to mix freely with people again. With Christ nothing is impossible. No heart-disease is so deep-seated but he is able to cure it. No plague of sin is so severe but the great physician can heal it. Never despair of anyone's salvation, so long as they live. The worst of spiritual lepers may yet be cleansed. Men are not lost because they are too bad to be saved, but because they will not come to Christ that he may save them.

Lastly, see that *there is a time to be silent about the work of Christ, as well as a time to speak*. This truth is taught here in a remarkable way. We read that 'Jesus sternly charged him and sent him away at once, and said to him, "See that you say nothing to anyone."' However, the man 'went out and began to talk freely about it, and to spread the news'—the result of which was 'that Jesus could no longer openly enter a town, but was in desolate places'.

Here is the lesson. There are times when our Lord would have us work for him quietly and silently, rather than attract public attention by a noisy zeal. There is 'a zeal for God, but not according to knowledge' (Romans 10:2), as well as a zeal which is righteous and praiseworthy. Our Master's cause may on some occasions be more advanced by quietness and patience, than in any other way. This is a delicate and difficult subject, and no doubt the majority of Christians are more inclined to be silent about their glorious Master than to confess him before men. But still it is undeniable that there is a time for all things—and to know the time should be one great aim of the Christian. Let us all pray for the Spirit of wisdom, seeking daily to know the path of duty.

Chapter 2

2:1–12

In these verses our Lord is at Capernaum once more, doing his accustomed work—preaching the word and healing the sick.

See first of all, *what great spiritual privileges some people enjoy, and yet make no use of them.* This truth is strikingly illustrated by the history of Capernaum, which seems to have enjoyed more of Jesus' presence during his earthly ministry than any city in Palestine. Here he dwelt after leaving Nazareth. Here many of his miracles were performed and much of his teaching delivered. Yet nothing that he said or did seems to have had any effect upon the hearts of the inhabitants, even though in this passage we are told that 'many were gathered together, so that there was no more room, not even at the door'. Though, after the present miracle, 'they were all amazed and glorified God', they were not converted. And Matthew 11:23–24 records the heaviest condemnation upon them from Jesus.

It is good for us all to mark well this case of Capernaum. We forget the amazing power of unbelief, and the depth of man's hostility against God. We need reminding that the same gospel which is the fragrance of life to some is the fragrance of death to others (2 Corinthians 2:15–16), and that the same fire which softens the wax will also harden the clay. Never was there a people so highly favoured as those of Capernaum, and never one who appear to have become so hard. Let us beware of walking in their steps.

See secondly, *how great a blessing affliction may prove to someone's soul.* We are told how 'a paralytic' [a person who was paralysed] was brought to Jesus. He was 'carried by four men', being helpless to come on his own. They made an opening in the roof and 'let down the bed on which the paralytic lay'. Jesus, the great physician of soul and body, saw him and gave him speedy relief. He restored him to health and strength and granted him also the far greater blessing of forgiveness of sins. The man 'rose and immediately picked up his bed and went out before them all'.

That paralysis was indeed a blessing. Without it he might have lived and died in ignorance, never have seen Christ, and never have heard the blessed words, 'My son, your sins are forgiven.' How many in every age can testify that this man's experience has been their own! Bereavements have proved mercies, losses have proved real gains, and sicknesses have led them to Jesus. Thousands can say with the psalmist, 'It is good for me that I was afflicted, that I might learn your statutes' (Psalm 119:71). So let us beware of murmuring under affliction. Every sickness and sorrow is a gracious message from God, and is intended to call us nearer to him.

See thirdly, *the priestly power of forgiving sins which is possessed by our Lord Jesus Christ*. When he spoke the words of forgiveness to the man, he uttered them with a meaning. Knowing the hearts of the scribes who were present he intended to show them his claim to be the true High Priest who has the power of pardoning sinners. He said to them, 'the Son of Man [Jesus himself] has authority on earth to forgive sins'. This is something that only God can do. No angel, no man, no church, no council, no minister can remove from the sinner's conscience the load of guilt, and give him peace with God.

How great a blessing it is to have Jesus as our great High Priest—he who is mighty to forgive and pardon, he who is tender-hearted and willing to save. So let us ask ourselves: have we yet known the Lord Jesus as our High Priest? Have we come to him and asked for forgiveness? If not, we are still in our sins. May we never rest until the Spirit bears witness with our spirit that we have sat at the feet of Jesus and heard his voice, saying, 'your sins are forgiven'.

2:13–22

Levi, the man we meet here, is the same man who is called Matthew in the first of the four Gospels. It is no less than an apostle and an evangelist whose early history is now before our eyes.

We learn from these verses, *the power of Christ to call men out from the world and make them his disciples*. Levi was 'sitting at the tax-booth' when

Jesus said to him, 'Follow me'. Immediately 'he rose and followed him'. From being a tax-collector, Levi became an apostle, and a writer of the first book in the New Testament, which is now known all over the world.

This is a truth of deep importance. Without a divine call, no one can be saved. We are all so sunk in sin, and so wedded to the world, that we should never turn to God and seek salvation, unless he first called us by his grace. God must speak to our hearts by his Spirit before we shall ever speak to him. When the Lord Jesus calls a sinner to be his servant, he acts as a sovereign; but he acts with infinite mercy, often choosing those who seem most unlikely to do his will and furthest off from his kingdom. He draws them to himself with almighty power, breaks the chains of old habits and customs, and makes them new creatures.

We should never despair entirely of anyone's salvation, when we read this passage of Scripture. He who called Levi, still lives and works. So let us hope continually and pray for others. Who can tell what God may be going to do for any one around us?

Learn also, that *one of Christ's principal offices is that of a physician.* The scribes and Pharisees found fault with Jesus for 'eating with sinners and tax-collectors'. However, 'when Jesus heard it, he said to them, "Those who are well have no need of a physician, but those who are sick."'

The Lord Jesus did not come into the world to be only a law-giver, teacher or example, but to be a physician as well. He knew the necessities of human nature. He saw us all sick of a mortal disease, stricken with the plague of sin. He pitied us, and came to bring divine medicine for our relief. He came to give health and cure to the dying, to heal the brokenhearted, and to offer strength to the weak. No sin-sick soul is too far gone for him.

But what do we know ourselves of this special office of Christ? Have we ever felt our spiritual sickness and applied to him for relief? We are never right in the sight of God until we do. To feel our sins and know our sickness is the first symptom of spiritual health. Apply to him without delay.

Learn finally, that *in religion it is worse than useless to attempt to mix things which essentially differ.* Jesus tells the Pharisees, 'No one sews a piece of unshrunk cloth on an old garment', and 'no one puts new wine into old wineskins.'

These words were a parable, spoken with reference to the question which had just been raised with him, as to why the disciples of John and of the Pharisees fasted, while Jesus' own disciples did not. His reply means that fasting might well be suitable for the disciples of him [John] who was the bridegroom's friend, but was not suitable for those disciples who actually had the bridegroom himself [Jesus] with them. To insist otherwise would be putting 'new wine into old wineskins'.

This is something of widespread application, forgetfulness of which can do great harm. For example, those to whom Paul wrote the letter to the Galatians sought to reconcile Judaism with Christianity by attempting to keep alive the old laws of ceremonies and ordinances and place them alongside the gospel of Christ. As for the present day, many professing Christians seek to reconcile the service of Christ with the service of the world, to have the name of Christian and yet live the life of the ungodly. All such are trying to enjoy the 'new wine' and yet cling to the 'old wineskins', or to sew a new patch 'on an old garment'. They will find that they have attempted that which cannot be done. 'No one can serve two masters' (Matthew 6:24).

2:23–28

We have here a remarkable scene in our Lord Jesus Christ's earthly ministry. We find him and his disciples 'going through the grainfields' on the Sabbath day, and are told that 'as they made their way, his disciples began to pluck heads of grain'. At once the Pharisees accused them to Jesus of 'doing what is not lawful on the Sabbath'.

Learn firstly, *what extravagant importance is attached to trifles by those who are mere formalists in religion*. The Pharisees were such, and seem only to have thought of the outward and ceremonial part of religion, even adding to these externals by traditions of their own. Their godliness was made up of such things as washings, fastings and peculiarities in dress, while repentance, faith and holiness were comparatively overlooked. They might have found no fault with Jesus' disciples over guilt in larger matters, such as offences against the moral law [the ten commandments], but the moment they saw an infringement on their own man-made traditions about the right way of keeping the Sabbath, they raised an outcry.

Let us watch and pray, lest we fall into the error of the Pharisees. There are always Christians to be found who walk in their steps, thinking more of the outward ceremonies of religion than of its doctrines. To do this is a symptom of spiritual disease, particularly when regard for man-made rites and ceremonies is exalted above the preaching of the gospel.

Learn secondly, *the value of a knowledge of holy Scripture*. Jesus replies to the Pharisees' accusation with a reference to Scripture. He reminds them of David's conduct, 'when he was in need and was hungry'. 'Have you never read what David did?', Jesus asks them. And what had David done? He had 'entered the house of God', and had eaten 'the bread of the Presence, which it is not lawful for any but the priests to eat'—thus showing that some requirements of God's laws might be relaxed in case of necessity.

The conduct of our Lord on this occasion ought to be a pattern for all his people. Our grand reason for faith and practice should always be, 'what does the Scripture say?' (Romans 4:3). We should endeavour to have the word of God on our side in all debatable questions. We should seek to be able to give a scriptural answer for our behaviour in all matters of dispute. We should refer our opponents to the Bible as our rule.

Let us remember, however, that if we are to use the Bible as our Lord did, we must know it well and be acquainted with its contents. We must read it diligently, humbly, perseveringly and prayerfully, or we shall never find its texts coming to our aid in the time of need. To use the sword of the Spirit effectually, we must be familiar with it and have it often in our hands. It is the students of the Bible, and they only, who will find it a weapon ready to hand in the day of battle.

Learn finally, *the true principle by which all questions about the observance of the Sabbath ought to be decided*. 'The Sabbath', Jesus declares, 'was made for man, not man for the Sabbath.' There is a mine of deep wisdom in those words, which are only recorded here out of the four Gospels.

'The Sabbath was made for man.' God made it for Adam in paradise, and renewed it to Israel on Mount Sinai. It was made for all mankind, not only for the Jews, and was made for man's benefit and happiness. It was for the good of his body, his mind and his soul. It was given to him as a blessing and not as a burden. This was the original institution. Yet this was not intended to prevent acts of mercy being done on that day.

There is nothing at all here to warrant the rash assertion of some, that our Lord has done away with the fourth commandment ['Remember the Sabbath day, to keep it holy', Exodus 20:8]. On the contrary, he manifestly speaks of the Sabbath day as a privilege and gift, never saying a word to justify the notion that Christians need not obey that commandment.

There is little danger of the day being kept too strictly in the present age. There is far more danger of it being profaned and forgotten entirely. Let us contend earnestly for its preservation among us in all its integrity. We may rest assured that national prosperity and personal growth in grace are intimately bound up in the maintenance of a holy Sabbath.

The concluding words of Jesus here, 'So the Son of Man is lord even of the Sabbath', declare that the Sabbath is his day—they clearly imply his own deity, for the Lord of the Sabbath day could be no less than God himself—and they state his intention of altering the day of rest from the seventh day of the week to the first [which was the day of the week upon which he would rise from the dead].

Chapter 3

3:1–12

These verses show us our Lord again working a miracle. He heals a man in the synagogue who 'was there with a withered hand'. Always about his Father's business—always doing good—doing it in the sight of enemies as well as friends—such was the daily character of Jesus' earthly ministry. And he left us 'an example, so that (we) might follow in his steps' (1 Peter 2:21). Blessed indeed are those Christians who strive, however feebly, to imitate their Master!

Observe firstly, *how our Lord Jesus Christ was watched by his enemies.* We are told that 'they watched Jesus, to see whether he would heal him on the Sabbath, so that they might accuse him'. What a proof of the wickedness of human nature! It was on the Sabbath day when these things happened, and in the synagogue, where people were assembled to worship God. The very men who pretended to such strictness and holiness in little things, were full of malicious and angry thoughts in the midst of the congregation.

Christ's people must not expect to fare better than their Master. They are always watched, their conduct is scanned, their ways are noted. They are marked people who can do nothing without the world noticing. If at any time they fall into an error, the ungodly rejoice. It is good for all Christians to keep this before their minds. The thought should make us exercise a holy jealousy over all our conduct, that we may do nothing to cause the enemy to blaspheme. It should make us pray much to be kept in our tempers, tongues and daily public behaviour. The Saviour who himself was watched, knows how to sympathise with his people, and to supply grace to help in time of need.

Observe secondly, *the great principle that our Lord lays down about Sabbath observance.* He teaches that it is 'lawful to do good' on the Sabbath. This principle is taught by a remarkable question. He asks those around him, 'Is it lawful on the Sabbath to do good or to do harm, to save life or to kill?' Was it better for him to heal the man with the withered hand, or to leave him alone? Was it more sinful to restore a person to health on the Sabbath than to commit murder? Was he to be blamed for saving a life on the Sabbath? No wonder that faced with such a question 'they were silent'.

It is plain from Jesus' words that no Christian need ever hesitate to do a really good work on the Lord's Day—such as ministering to the sick or relieving pain. The holiness with which the fourth commandment invests the Sabbath day is not in the least degree invaded by anything of this kind. But we must take care that the principle Jesus lays down here is not abused. The permission 'to do good' does not mean doing as we please on this day. It was never intended to open the door to amusements, journeying or sensual gratification.

Observe thirdly, *the feelings which the conduct of our Lord's enemies called forth in his heart*. We read that 'he looked around at them with anger, grieved at their hardness of heart'. This demands our special attention, for it is meant to remind us that our Lord Jesus Christ was a man like ourselves in all things, with the one exception of sin. So whatever sinless feelings belong to man, our Lord partook of them and knew them in his own experience.

It is plain from these words that there is an anger which is right and not sinful, that there is an indignation which is justified on proper occasions. 'Be angry and do not sin' (Ephesians 4:26). Yet of all the feelings that people experience there is none perhaps which so soon runs into sin as the feeling of anger. The length to which ill-temper, irritability and passion will carry even godly men, all must know. The awful fact that passionate words are a breach of the sixth commandment is taught plainly by Jesus in the Sermon on the Mount. A sinless wrath is a very rare thing. The wrath of man is seldom for the glory of God. Nevertheless, we learn here that there is an anger which is lawful. And in every case a righteous indignation should be mingled with grief and sorrow for those who cause it, even as it was in the case of our Lord.

3:13–21

The beginning of this passage describes the appointment of the twelve apostles. What vast benefit these few men have conferred on the world. Their names are known while the names of many kings and rich men are forgotten.

Notice here, *how many of the twelve who are here named had been called to be disciples before they were ordained apostles.* There are at least six of them whose first call to follow Christ is recorded (Peter and Andrew, James and John, Philip and Matthew). There can be little doubt that eleven of Jesus' apostles were converted before they were ordained. It ought to be the same with all ministers of the gospel. They ought to be men who have been first called by the Spirit, before they are set apart for the great work of teaching others.

It is impossible to overrate the importance of this. An unconverted minister is utterly unfit for his office. How can he speak from experience of that grace which he has never tasted himself? How can he commend that Saviour to his people who he himself only knows by name? How can he urge on souls the need of that conversion and new birth which he himself has not experienced?

Notice secondly, *the nature of the office to which the apostles were ordained.* They were to 'be with' Jesus. They were to be sent out 'to preach'. They were to 'have authority to cast out demons'. They were undoubtedly a distinct order of men, who had no successors when they died. However, we must not forget that in many things they were intended to be patterns and models for all ministers of the gospel. With this in mind, we may draw useful lessons from this passage as to the duties of a faithful minister.

Like the apostles, the faithful minister ought to keep up close communion with Christ. He should be much 'with him'. He should abide in him, be separate from the world, sit at his feet, and hear his word. He should be able to say, when he enters the pulpit to preach, 'that which we have seen and heard we proclaim also to you' (1 John 1:3).

Like the apostles, the faithful minister ought to be a preacher. This must always be his principal work. Like them, he must labour to do good in very way, striving (although he cannot heal the sick) to be the comforter, counsellor, peacemaker, helper and friend of all, being their servant 'for Jesus' sake' (2 Corinthians 4:5). Like them, he must oppose every work of the devil, constantly ready (though not called now to cast out evil spirits from the body) to resist the devil's devices and to denounce his snares for the soul.

How great is the responsibility of ministers. How heavy their work, if they do their duty. How they need the prayers of all praying people. No wonder the apostle Paul says to the church, 'Brothers, pray for us' (1 Thessalonians 5:25).

Notice in the third place, *how our Lord Jesus Christ's zeal was misunderstood by his enemies*. We are told that 'they went out to seize him, for they were saying, "He is out of his mind."'

There is nothing in this that need surprise us. Few things show the corruption of human nature more clearly than man's inability to understand zeal in religion. Zeal about money, or science, or war, or commerce, or business makes sense to the world. But zeal in religion is too often considered foolishness, fanaticism, and the sign of a weak mind. Festus said to Paul, 'Paul, you are out of your mind' (Acts 26:24). The 'things of the Spirit of God' are always 'folly' to the unbeliever (1 Corinthians 2:14).

Let it not shake our faith, if we have to drink of the same cup as our blessed Lord. Hard as it may be to us to be misunderstood by our relatives, we must recall that it is no new thing. Let us call to mind Jesus' words, 'Whoever loves father or mother more than me is not worthy of me' (Matthew 10:37). Jesus knows the bitterness of our trials, feels for us, and will give us help. Let us bear patiently the unreasonableness of unconverted men, even as he did, pitying their blindness and lack of knowledge, not loving them any less, and praying that God will change their hearts.

3:22–30

We all know how painful it is to have our conduct misunderstood and misrepresented, when we are doing right. It is a trial which our Lord Jesus Christ had to endure throughout his earthly ministry, and we have an instance of it in the passage before us. We read of 'the scribes who came down from Jerusalem', who, although they had seen Jesus' miracles and could not deny their reality, accused him of being in league with the devil. They said, 'He is possessed by Beelzebul' and 'by the prince of demons he casts out the demons.'

Notice firstly, from Jesus' answer, *how great is the evil of dissensions and divisions*. This lesson is brought out in the beginning of Jesus' reply to the scribes. He shows how absurd it is to suppose that Satan would 'cast out Satan', and so help to destroy his own power. He appeals to the fact (which even his enemies must allow) that there can be no strength where there is division. 'If a kingdom is divided against itself, that kingdom cannot stand.'

This is a truth which does not receive sufficient consideration. The divisions of Christians are one great cause of the weakness of the visible church. They often absorb energy and time which might well have been bestowed on better things. They furnish the unbeliever with a prime argument against the truth of Christianity. They help the devil, who is the chief promoter of such divisions. If he cannot extinguish Christianity, he labours to make Christians quarrel with one another.

Let us resolve, so far as in us lies, to avoid all differences, dissensions and disputes among Christians. We cannot be too jealous about all saving truths, but it is easy to mistake zeal about trifles for zeal about the truth. Nothing justifies separation from a church but the separation of that church from the gospel.

Notice secondly, *what a glorious declaration our Lord makes in these verses about the forgiveness of sins*. He says, 'all sins shall be forgiven the children of man, and whatever blasphemies they utter'.

These words fall lightly on the ears of many people who see no particular beauty in them. But to those who are alive to their own sinfulness and deeply conscious of their need of mercy, these words are sweet and precious. That 'all sins shall be forgiven', includes the sins of youth and age—the sins of head, hand, tongue and imagination—the sins of persecutors (like Saul), idolaters (like Manasseh), open enemies of Christ (like those who crucified him), and backsliders from Christ (like Peter). The blood of Christ can cleanse all away. The righteousness of Christ can cover all, and hide all from God's eyes.

The doctrine here laid down is the crown and glory of the gospel, for it promises free pardon and full forgiveness, 'without money and without price' (Isaiah 55:1). Let us lay hold upon it without delay, if we have never received it before. We too, this very day, if we come to Christ, may be completely forgiven; 'though (our) sins are like scarlet, they shall be as white as snow' (Isaiah 1:18). And, if we have already received it, let us cleave firmly to it. We may sometimes feel faint, unworthy and cast down—but if we have truly come to Jesus by faith, our sins are forgiven. They are cast behind God's back, blotted out of his book of remembrance, sunk into the depths of the sea. Let us believe and not be afraid.

Notice lastly, *that it is possible for a man's soul to be lost for ever in hell.* Jesus' words are very clear when he speaks of one who 'never has forgiveness, but is guilty of an eternal sin'. Without doubt, this is an awful truth, and we must not shut our eyes against it. We find it asserted over and over again in Scripture. Teachers continue to rise up and openly attack the doctrine of eternal punishment, or seek to explain it away. They speak of the impossibility of a loving God permitting an everlasting hell.

Let us hold firmly to the old truth Jesus asserts here. Let us not be ashamed to believe that there is an eternal God, an eternal heaven, and an eternal hell. Let us recollect that sin is an infinite evil, needing an atonement of infinite value to deliver the believer from its consequences—and involving an infinite loss on the unbeliever who rejects the remedy provided for it. Let us escape for our lives and not linger. Let us flee for refuge to the hope set before us in the gospel, and never rest until we know and feel that we are safe.

Before leaving this passage, there is an expression within it which demands special notice. It is one of the hard things of Scripture, and has often troubled the hearts of Bible readers. Jesus states that, 'whoever blasphemes against the Holy Spirit never has forgiveness, but is guilty of an eternal sin'. What is this unpardonable sin? Some say that the assertion by the scribes who (having witnessed Jesus' miracles, yet having refused to believe in him as the Messiah) maintained that he worked those miracles through Beelzebul, was blasphemy against the Holy Spirit. The most probable view is that it is a combination of clear intellectual knowledge of the gospel, with deliberate rejection of it and wilful choice of sin. It is a union of light in the head and hatred in the heart—such was the case of Judas Iscariot. Yet the limits which knowledge combined with unbelief must pass, in order to become the unpardonable sin, are graciously withheld from us.

But although it is difficult to define what the unpardonable sin is, it is far less difficult to point out what it is not. A few words on this point may possibly help to relieve tender consciences. We may lay it down as nearly certain, that those who are troubled with fears that they have committed this sin are the very people who have not done so. The very fact that they are afraid and anxious about it is the strongest possible evidence in their favour. A troubled conscience—an anxiety about salvation, and a dread of being cast away—a concern about the next world, and a desire to escape from the wrath of God—these things will probably never be found in the heart of that person who has sinned the sin for which there is no forgiveness. It is far more probable that the general marks of such a person will be utter hardness of conscience—a seared heart, causing an absence of any feeling—a thorough insensibility to spiritual concern. The subject may safely be left there.

3:31–35

In these verses we find that the charge of the scribes against Jesus, just considered, was not all that he had to endure at this time. We are told that 'his mother and his brothers came, and standing outside they sent to him and called him'. They could not yet understand the beauty and usefulness of the life that he was living, though doubtless they loved him well.

We learn from these verses one mighty lesson: *who they are who are reckoned the relations of Jesus Christ*. They are those who are his disciples and do 'the will of God'. Of such, the great Head of the church says, 'Whoever does the will of God, he is my brother and sister and mother.'

How much there is in this single expression! What a rich mine of consolation it opens to all true believers! Who can conceive the depth of our Lord's love towards Mary, the mother who bare him, and on whose bosom he had been nursed? Who can imagine the breadth of his love towards his brethren according to the flesh, with whom the tender years of his childhood had been spent? Yet even so, he says of each person who 'does the will of God', that such 'is my brother and sister and mother'.

Let all true Christians drink comfort out of these words. Let them know that there is one at least, who knows them, loves them, cares for them, and reckons them as his own family. However poor they are in this world, however persecuted and ill-treated in their own homes because of their faith—they have no cause to be ashamed, for they are the brothers and sisters of the Son of God. They may remember the words of David, and apply them to their own case: 'For my father and my mother have forsaken me, but the LORD will take me in' (Psalm 27:10).

Finally, let all who persecute and ridicule others because of their faith in Jesus, take warning by these words and repent. Who are they persecuting and ridiculing? The relations of Jesus the Son of God! The family of the King of kings and Lord of lords! Surely they do wisely to hold their peace and consider well that they are doing. Those whom they treat in this way have a mighty Friend: 'for their Redeemer is strong; he will plead their cause' (Proverbs 23:11).

Chapter 4

4:1–20

These verses contain the parable of the sower. Of all Jesus' parables, this is probably the best known. Its language requires no explanation.

We are taught, first of all, *that there are some hearers of the gospel whose hearts are like the wayside in the field*. These are those people who hear sermons, but pay no attention to them. They attend a place of worship, but take no interest in the preaching. Whether it is the law or the gospel, it produces no more effect on them than water on a stone. At the end, they go away knowing no more than when they came in.

There are countless professing Christians in this state of soul. Week after week, they allow the devil to snatch away the good seed that is sown on the face of their hearts. They live on, without faith, fear, knowledge or grace—feeling and caring nothing, taking no more interest than if Christ had never died on the cross at all. And in this state they often die, are buried, and are lost for ever in hell. This is a mournful picture, but only too true.

We are taught, secondly, *that there are some hearers of the gospel whose hearts are like the stony ground in a field*. These are they on whom preaching produces temporary impressions, but no deep or lasting effect. They take pleasure in hearing sermons in which the truth is faithfully set forth—they can speak with apparent enthusiasm about the sweetness of the gospel—they can be moved to tears by the appeals of preachers, and speak with apparent earnestness of their own inward conflicts, hopes, struggles, desires and fears. But they have no stability about their religion, for 'they have no root in themselves, but endure for a while'. There is no real work of the Holy Spirit in their hearts. They fade as rapidly as they grow. As soon as 'tribulation or persecution arises on account of the word, immediately they fall away'.

Again, there are many in every congregation which hears the gospel, who are just in this state of soul. They feel a pleasure in what they hear and therefore flatter themselves that they must have grace in their hearts; yet they are thoroughly deceived. Old things have not passed away. They are actually on the high road to destruction.

We are taught, thirdly, *that there are some hearers of the gospel whose hearts are like the thorny ground in a field*. They attend to the preaching of Christ's truth, and to a certain extent they obey it. Their understanding assents to it, their judgment approves of it, their conscience is affected by it. They acknowledge that it is right and good, and worthy of acceptance. They even abstain from many things which the gospel condemns, and adopt many habits which the gospel requires. But here they stop short. And this is why: 'the cares of the world and the deceitfulness of riches and the desires for other things enter in and choke the word, and it proves unfruitful'.

They go so far and yet go no further. They approve so much and yet will not give Christ their heart. And there is but one verdict that can be given about such people: without a decided change they will never enter the kingdom of heaven. 'Therefore whoever wishes to be a friend of the world makes himself an enemy of God' (James 4:4).

We are taught, fourthly, *that there are some hearers of the gospel whose hearts are like the good ground in a field*. These are those people who really receive Christ's truth into their hearts, believe it unquestioningly, and obey it thoroughly. In these, the fruits of that truth will be seen— sin will be truly hated, mourned over, resisted and renounced. Christ will be truly loved, trusted in, followed and obeyed. Holiness will show itself in all their conversation, in humility, spiritual-mindedness, patience, meekness and love. There will be something that can be seen, for the true work of the Holy Spirit cannot be hid.

There will always be some people in this state of soul, where the gospel is faithfully preached. Their numbers may be few, compared to the worldly around them. Their experience and degree of spiritual attainment may differ widely (some bringing forth thirty, some sixty and some a hundredfold). But there will always be, in all of them, visible repentance, visible faith in Christ, and visible holiness of life. Without these things, there is no saving religion.

So let us ask ourselves: what are we? Under which class of hearers ought we to be ranked? With what kind of hearts do we hear the word? Never forget that there are three ways of hearing without profit, and only one way of hearing rightly! Never forget that there is only one sure mark of being a right-hearted hearer, and that is to bear fruit. To be without fruit is to be in the way to hell.

4:21–25

These verses seem intended to enforce the parable of the sower on the attention of those who heard it. It is noteworthy that this passage is one among many proofs that Jesus used the same words and the same ideas on many different occasions.

First of all, we learn *that we ought not only to receive knowledge, but impart it to others*. A lamp is not lit to be hidden away, but to be set upon a stand and used. Spiritual light is not given to anyone for themselves alone, but for the benefit of others. We are to try and spread what we know, displaying to others the precious treasure we have found, and persuading them to seek it for themselves. We shall all have to give account of our use of knowledge one day. 'For nothing is hidden except to be made manifest.'

All Christians should lay this to heart. To do good and diffuse light is a duty for which all members of Christ's church are responsible. Neighbours ought to tell neighbours, if they have found an unfailing remedy in time of plague. Christians ought to tell others that they have found medicine for their souls, if they see them ignorant, and dying for lack of it.

Secondly, we learn *the importance of hearing and of considering well what we hear*. This is a point to which our Lord evidently attaches great weight. Observe these two expressions: 'If anyone has ears to hear, let him hear' and 'Pay attention to what you hear.'

Hearing the truth is one principal avenue through which grace is conveyed to anyone's soul, for 'faith comes from hearing' (Romans 10:17). One of the first steps towards conversion is to receive from the Holy Spirit a hearing ear. Hearing God's word is one of the foremost means of grace that he has given to us.

Lastly, we learn *the importance of a diligent use of spiritual privileges*. What does Jesus say? 'For to the one who has, more will be given, and from the one who has not, even what he has will be taken away'.

This is a principle which we find continually brought forward in Scripture. All that believers possess is undoubtedly of grace. Repentance, faith and holiness are all the gift of God. But the degree to which a believer attains in grace is closely connected with his own diligence in the use of means, and his own faithfulness in living up fully to the light and knowledge which he has. Labour and pains in hearing, reading and prayer are always represented as bringing their own reward. It is declared that while 'the soul of the diligent is richly supplied' (Proverbs 13:4), yet 'an idle person will suffer hunger' (Proverbs 19:15). Attention to this is a key secret of spiritual prosperity. The growing Christian must always be diligent with the Bible, diligent in private devotions, diligent in hearing sermons, and diligent in attendance at the Lord's Table. He reaps according to how he sows. Just as the muscles of the body are strengthened by regular exercise, so the graces of the soul are increased by diligence in using them.

Do we wish to grow in grace? Do we desire to have stronger faith, brighter hope and clearer knowledge? Most certainly we do, if we are true Christians. Then let us live up to our light and improve every opportunity, for 'with the measure you use, it will be measured to you'.

4:26–29

The parable recorded here is short, and only recorded in Mark's Gospel. It is one of deep interest to all who have reason to hope they are true Christians. It sets before us the history of the work of grace in an individual soul, and summons us to an examination of our own experience in divine things. The main thing taught is the close resemblance between some familiar operations in the growth of grain and the work of grace in the heart.

Firstly, as in the growth of grain, so in the work of grace, *there must be a sower*. The seed must be scattered or there would never be a harvest;

for, left to itself, the ground would bring forth only weeds. Similarly, the heart of man will never of itself produce repentance, faith and obedience. It is entirely dead towards God, and unable to give itself spiritual life. It must be broken up by the Holy Spirit and given a new nature. The good seed of the word must be scattered upon it.

Grace in anyone's heart is a new principle from outside, sent down from heaven and implanted in the soul. Otherwise no one would ever seek God. Yet God ordinarily works by means, as preachers and teachers 'sow' the word of truth.

Secondly, as in the growth of grain, so in the work of grace, *there is much that is beyond man's comprehension and control*. The wisest farmer in the world can never explain all that takes place in a grain of wheat once he has sown it. He knows that unless he puts it into the ground, there will be no ear of grain when harvest comes. But he cannot explain why some grains come up and others die, neither can he specify the hour or minute when life will begin to show itself. These are matters he must leave alone.

The workings of grace in the heart, likewise, are utterly mysterious and unsearchable. We cannot explain why the word produces different effects upon different people, as some reject it and continue dead in their trespasses and sins, while others are born again and become decided Christians. We cannot define the manner in which the Spirit of God conveys life to a soul, and the exact process by which a believer receives a new nature. All these things are hidden to us. 'The wind blows where it wishes, and you hear its sound, but you do not know where it comes from or where it goes. So it is with everyone who is born of the Spirit' (John 3:8). Only God can give life. Our principal work is to sow the seed. That done, we wait with faith and patience for the result.

Thirdly, as in the growth of grain, so in the work of grace, *life manifests itself gradually*. The ripe ear of wheat does not appear at once, as soon as the seed bursts into life. The plant goes through many stages before it arrives at perfection—'first the blade, then the ear, then the full grain in the ear'. But in all these stages one great thing is true about it—even at its weakest, it is a living plant.

In such a manner, the work of grace goes on in the heart by degrees. The children of God are not born perfect in faith, or hope, or knowledge, or experience. They see only in part their own sinfulness, Christ's fullness, and the beauty of holiness. Yet for all that, the weakest child in God's family is a true child of God. With all his weakness and infirmity, he is alive. The seed of grace has truly come up in his heart, though at present it be only in the blade.

There is great consolation here. Let us never despise grace, just because it is weak. Always remember that grace, like everything else, must have a beginning. The mightiest oak was once an acorn. The strongest man was once a baby. Better a thousand times have grace in the blade than have no grace at all.

Lastly, as in the growth of grain, so in the work of grace, *there is no harvest until the seed is ripe.* No farmer thinks of cutting his wheat when it is green. He waits for the sun and rain, the heat and cold, to have done their appointed work, and for the golden ears to hang down. Only then, 'when the grain is ripe, at once he puts in the sickle, because the harvest has come'.

God deals with his work of grace in exactly the same way. He never removes his people from this world before they are ripe and ready and their work is done. They never die at the wrong time, however mysterious their deaths sometimes appear to us. The Great Husbandman never cuts his grain until it is ripe. So let this comfort us about the death of every believer. There is no chance, no accident, no mistake about the death of any of God's children. He always knows best when they are ready for the harvest.

4:30–34

This parable of the mustard seed is one of those parables which have the character both of history and prophecy. It appears to illustrate the history of Christ's visible church on earth, from the time of his coming into the world until the judgment day. The seed cast into the ground in the preceding parable showed the work of grace in a heart. The mustard seed shows the progress of professing Christianity in the world.

We learn, firstly, that like the grain of mustard seed, *Christ's visible church was to be small and weak in its beginnings.* A grain of mustard seed was a proverbial expression among the Jews for something very small and insignificant. Jesus calls it 'the smallest of all the seeds on earth'. Twice in the Gospels Jesus uses it as a word of comparison, when speaking of a weak faith.

It would be difficult to find a picture which more faithfully represents the history of the visible church than this grain of mustard seed. Weakness and apparent insignificance were undoubtedly the characteristics of its beginning. Jesus, though Head and King, came into the world as a feeble infant, born in a manger at Bethlehem, without riches, armies, attendants or power. Those whom he gathered around himself and appointed as apostles were poor and unlearned people, to all appearance the most unlikely folk to shake the world. In his death on the cross, Jesus was crucified between two criminals, having been forsaken by nearly all his disciples, betrayed by one, and denied by another. The doctrine which the early church preached was 'a stumbling block to Jews and folly to Gentiles' (1 Corinthians 1:23).

We learn, secondly, that like the mustard seed, *the visible church, once planted, was to grow and greatly increase.* Jesus says of it, 'when it is sown it grows up and becomes larger than all the garden plants'. This illustrates very strikingly the growth and increase of Christ's visible church in the world. It began to grow from the day of Pentecost, and grew with a rapidity which can only be accounted for by the finger of God. It grew wonderfully when three thousand souls were converted at once, and many more were added in the days that followed—when congregations were established at Antioch, Ephesus, Philippi, Corinth and Rome—and when at last the despised religion of Christ spread over the greater part of Europe, Asia Minor and Africa, despite fierce opposition and persecution, and became the professed creed of the Roman empire. And it has not finished growing yet. The prophecy is far from exhausted.

A day shall yet come when the great Head of the church shall take to himself his power and reign, putting down every enemy under his feet. 'For the earth will be filled with the knowledge of the glory of the LORD as the waters cover the sea' (Habakkuk 2:14). The nations will yet be our Lord's 'heritage, and the ends of the earth (his) possession' (Psalm 2:8). The little seed which was planted has become a great tree, and we ourselves are rejoicing under its shadow. Let us never despise 'the day of small things' (Zechariah 4:10).

4:35–41

These verses describe a storm on the sea of Galilee, when Jesus and his disciples were crossing it—and a miracle which he performed in calming the storm in a moment. Few miracles recorded in the Gospels were so likely to strike the minds of the apostles as these, since four of them at least were fishermen (Peter, Andrew, James and John). No doubt they would have known this water and its storms from their youth.

The first thing for us to learn here is, *that Christ's service does not exempt his servants from storms*. Here were the twelve disciples in the path of duty, obediently following Jesus wherever he went. Yet here they were in trouble, tossed up and down by a tempest and in danger of being drowned.

This teaches us that if we are true Christians, we must not expect everything to be smooth in our journey to heaven. We must not count it a strange thing if we have to endure sickness, loss, bereavement and disappointment, just like everybody else. Free pardon and full forgiveness, grace along the way and glory at the end—all this our Saviour has promised to give. But he has never promised that we shall have no affliction. He loves us too well to promise that, for he teaches us many precious lessons through affliction, which we would never learn without it. He shows us our emptiness and weakness, draws us to the throne of grace, purifies our affections, weans us from the world, and makes us long for heaven. In the resurrection morning, we shall all say, 'It is good for me that I was afflicted' (Psalm 119:71). We shall thank God for every storm.

The second thing for us to learn here is, *that our Lord Jesus Christ was really and truly man*. We are told that when the storm began 'and the waves were breaking into the boat', Jesus 'was in the stern, asleep on the cushion'. He had a body exactly like our own—one that could hunger and thirst, feel pain and be weary, and need rest. No wonder that as evening had come, and having been busily about his Father's business all day, he fell asleep.

The Saviour in whom we trust is as really a man as he is God. He knows our trials, for he has experienced them. He knows our bodily infirmities, for he has felt them. He can well understand what we mean when we cry to him for help in this world of need. He is the very Saviour we need for our comfort every morning and night. 'For we do not have a high priest who is unable to sympathise with our weaknesses' (Hebrews 4:15).

The third thing for us to learn is, *that our Lord Jesus Christ, as God, has almighty power*. He speaks to the wind, and it obeys him. He speaks to the sea, and it submits to his command. He turns the raging storm into a calm with a few words: 'Peace! Be still!' Those were the words of him who first created all things. The wind and the sea knew the voice of their Master, and, like obedient servants, were quiet at once.

With the Lord Jesus Christ, nothing is impossible. He can tame stormy passions—he can change violent tempers—he can speak peace to disquieted consciences. No one need ever despair, if he will only bow down his pride, and come as a humbled sinner to Jesus. No one need ever despair of reaching his journey's end, if he has once committed his soul to Christ's keeping. Whoever it may be who opposes us and however great our temptations may be, Christ is on our side, and we are in the boat with him. Greater is he who is for us, than all those who are against us.

The final thing for us to learn is, *that our Lord Jesus Christ is exceedingly patient and pitiful in dealing with his own people*. We see the disciples here showing great lack of faith and giving way to fears. They forgot their Master's miracles and care for them in days gone by. They thought of nothing but their present peril. So they awoke Jesus hastily, 'and said to him, "Teacher, do you not care that we are perishing?"' And we see him dealing most gently and tenderly with them. He gives them no sharp reproof because of their unbelief. He simply asks the touching question, 'Why are you so afraid? Have you still no faith?'

'As a father shows compassion to his children, so the LORD shows compassion to those who fear him' (Psalm 103:13). He does not deal with believers 'according to our sins', neither does he 'repay us according to our iniquities' (Psalm 103:10). He sees our weaknesses and is aware of our shortcomings. He knows all the defects of our faith, hope, love and courage. Yet he will not cast us off. He bears with us continually, loves us to the end, raises us when we fall, and restores us when we err.

Jesus has not changed. His heart is still the same as it was when he crossed the sea of Galilee and stilled the storm. High in heaven at the right hand of God, Jesus is still sympathising, still almighty, still pitiful and patient towards his people. So let us be more charitable and patient towards our brethren in the faith, for if Jesus has received them and bears with them, surely we must bear with them too. And let us be more hopeful about ourselves. We may be very weak, frail and unstable; but if we can truly say that we do to come to Christ and believe on him, we may take comfort.

Chapter 5

5:1–17

These verses describe one of those mysterious miracles which the Gospels frequently record—the casting out of a devil. Of all the cases of this kind described in the New Testament, none is so fully described as this one.

We see here, firstly, *that the possession of a man's body by the devil was a real and true thing in the time of our Lord's earthly ministry*. Sadly, there is never any shortage of professing Christians who try to explain away Jesus' miracles, and particularly those which involve the casting out of devils. They deny Satanic possession altogether, and declare the idea of the devil inhabiting someone's body to be absurd.

The best and simplest way to answer such sceptical objections, is to refer to the plain narratives of the Gospels, not least this present one. The facts detailed here cannot be explained if we do not believe in Satanic possession. No doubt there is much in this subject which we do not understand and cannot explain—but let us not therefore refuse to believe it. We may be sure, that upon the matter of the devil and his power, we are far more likely to believe too little than too much. Unbelief about the existence and personality of Satan has often proved the first step to unbelief about God.

We see here, secondly, *what an awfully cruel, powerful and malicious being Satan is*. All three of these characteristics are set forth here. Satan's *cruelty* appears in the miserable condition of the unhappy man, of whose body he had possession. We are told that the man 'lived among the tombs', that 'no one could bind him anymore, not even with a chain', that 'Night and day among the tombs and on the mountains he was always crying out and bruising himself with stones'. Such is the state to which the devil would bring us all, if only he could. He would rejoice to inflict upon us the utmost misery, both of body and mind. Cases like this are faint types of the miseries of hell.

Satan's *power* appears in the awful words which the unclean spirit used, when Jesus asked, 'What is your name?', he answered, 'My name is Legion, for we are many.' We probably do not have the faintest idea of the number, subtlety and activity of Satan's agents. In private and in public, in the church and in the world, there are busy enemies ever near us, of whose presence we are unaware.

Satan's *malice* appears in the strange petition, 'Send us to the pigs.' Cast forth from the man, whose body they had so long inhabited and possessed, they still thirsted to do mischief. Such is the true character of Satan. His whole nature is to do harm, kill and destroy.

Let us beware of the senseless habit of jesting about the devil. It is a habit which furnishes awful evidence of the blindness and corruption of human nature, and one which is far too common. Well would it be for us all, if we sought to realise the power and presence of our great spiritual enemy, and prayed more to be delivered from him.

We see here, lastly, *how complete is our Lord's power and authority over the devil.* We see it in the cry of the unclean spirit, 'I adjure you by God, do not torment me'—in the command, 'Come out of the man, you unclean spirit!', and the immediate obedience that followed—in the blessed change that at once took place in the man who had been possessed: he was found 'sitting there, clothed and in his right mind'—and in the petition of all the devils, 'Send us to the pigs; let us enter them', confessing their consciousness that they could do nothing without leave. All these things show that one mightier than Satan was there. Strong as the great enemy of man was, he was in the presence of one stronger than he.

The truth taught here is full of strong consolation for all true Christians. We live in a world full of difficulties and snares. We are ourselves weak and compassed with infirmity. The thought that we have such a mighty spiritual enemy ever near us might well fill us with disquiet. But, thanks be to God, we have in Jesus an almighty Friend, who 'is able to save to the uttermost' (Hebrews 7:25). He has already triumphed over Satan on the cross. He will ever triumph over him in the hearts of all believers, and intercede for them that their faith will not fail. And Jesus will finally triumph over Satan completely, at his second coming.

So: are we ourselves delivered from Satan's power? This is the grand question that concerns our souls. Have we, by grace, broken his bonds and escaped from his hands? Do we daily resist him and make him flee? Do we 'Put on the whole armour of God' (Ephesians 6:11) and stand against his schemes? May we never rest until we can give satisfactory answers to these questions.

5:18–20

What those people did after Jesus healed and cured them is a thing not often related in the Gospels. The account often describes the miraculous cure but then leaves the subsequent history of the person cured in obscurity, and passes on to other things. But there are some deeply interesting cases in which we do learn what happened with them afterwards, and the man here from whom the devil has been cast, is one.

We learn two things in particular from these verses. Firstly, *the Lord Jesus knows better than his people what is the right position for them to be in.* We are told that when our Lord was on the point of leaving the country of the Gerasenes, 'the man who had been possessed with demons begged him that he might be with him'. We can well understand that request. Feeling grateful for the blessed change that had taken place in himself, and being full of love towards his Deliverer, he thought he could not do better than follow Jesus and go with him as his companion and disciple. Yet, strange as it might at first appear, his request was refused. Jesus 'did not permit him', for he had other work for him to do. Jesus saw better than the man did in what way he could glorify God most. So Jesus 'said to him, "Go home to your friends and tell them how much the Lord has done for you, and how he has had mercy on you."'

There are lessons of profound wisdom in these words. The place that Christians wish to be in is not always the place that is best for their souls. The position that they would choose, if they could have their own way, is not always that which Jesus would have them occupy. Those who are newly converted need this lesson especially, but let us all pray that God would guide us in all our ways after conversion, and that he would not allow us to make wrong choices or hasty decisions.

The great thing is to have no will of our own, and to be where Jesus would have us be.

Secondly, *a believer's own home has the first claims on his attention.* We learn this from the striking words which Jesus addresses to the man here: 'Go home to your friends and tell them how much the Lord has done for you.' This man's friends had probably not seen him for some years, except him being under the influence of Satan. Here, then, was the path of duty. Here was the way by which he could most glorify God. Let him go home and tell his friends what Jesus had done for him. Let him be a living witness before their eyes of the compassion of Christ. Let him deny himself the pleasure of being in Christ's physical presence, in order to do the higher work of being useful to others.

How much there is in these simple words of our Lord. Home is the place above all others where the child of God ought to make his first endeavours to do good. Home is where he is seen continually, and where the reality of his grace ought most truly to appear. Home is the place where his best affections should be concentrated and where he should strive daily to witness for Christ.

If we have never yet been born again and made new creatures, we can of course have nothing to 'tell'. But if we do have anything to tell others about Christ, let us resolve to tell it. Let us not be silent if we have found peace and rest in the gospel. Let us speak to our relations, friends, families and neighbours, as we have opportunity, and tell them what the Lord has done for us. All are not called to be ministers or to preach, but all can walk in the steps of the man of whom we have been reading. Happy are those who are not ashamed to say to others, 'Come and hear, all you who fear God, and I will tell what he has done for my soul' (Psalm 66:16).

5:21–34

The main subject of these verses is the miraculous healing of a sick woman. Great is our Lord's experience in cases of disease. He is always set before us as gentle, easy to be entreated, the healer of the broken hearted, the refuge of the weak and helpless, the comforter of the distressed, the sick person's best friend. He is the very Saviour that human nature needs.

Five lessons are to be noted here. Firstly, *what misery sin has brought into the world*. We read of one who had had a most painful disease 'for twelve years'. She had 'suffered much under many physicians, and had spent all that she had, and was no better but rather grew worse'. Medical skill had been unable to cure her.

How remarkable it is that we do not hate sin more than we do, for sin is the cause of all the pain and disease in the world. God did not create man to be an ailing and suffering creature. Let us keep this ever in mind, and hate sin with a godly hatred.

Secondly, *how different are the feelings with which people draw near to Christ*. We are told that 'a great crowd followed him and thronged about him'. But we are only told of one person who 'came up behind him in the crowd and touched him' with faith and was healed. Many followed Jesus from curiosity, and derived no benefit from him. One, and only one, followed him under a deep sense of need, and of our Saviour's power to relieve her, and that one received a mighty blessing.

The same thing can happen in our own day. Fashion, custom, form, habit, the love of excitement, or an itching ear, can be the motives of many. There are comparatively few who touch Christ by faith and go home 'in peace'.

Thirdly, *how immediate and instantaneous was the cure which this woman received*. No sooner did she touch Jesus' clothes than she was healed. The thing that she had sought in vain for twelve years, was done in a moment. The cure that many physicians could not effect, was wrought in an instant of time. 'And immediately the flow of blood dried up, and she felt in her body that she was healed of her disease.'

We need not doubt that we are intended to see here an emblem of the relief that the gospel confers upon souls. The experience of many a weary conscience has been exactly like that of this woman with her disease. Many have spent sorrowful years in search of peace with God, and failed to find it. Earthly remedies have brought no relief, and after going from church to church they have ended up worse rather than better. But at last rest has been found—and where? They have found it where this woman found hers—in Jesus Christ. They have ceased from their own works, and have come to Christ himself, as humble sinners, and cast themselves upon his mercy. At once, the burden has fallen off their shoulders, heaviness is turned to joy, and anxiety to peace. Personal application to Christ is the real secret of peace with God.

Fourthly, *how much it becomes Christians to confess before men the benefit they receive from Christ.* This woman was not allowed to go home, when cured, without her cure being noticed. Jesus inquired who had touched him, and 'turned about in the crowd, and said, "Who touched my garments?"' No doubt he knew perfectly the name and history of the woman, and did not need anyone to tell him. But he desired to teach her, and everyone around him, that healed souls should make public acknowledgment of mercies received.

Here is a lesson for all true Christians to remember. We are not to be ashamed to confess Christ before men, and to let others know what he has done for our souls. If we have found peace through his blood, and been renewed by his Spirit, we must not shrink from confessing it openly. If we are ashamed of Jesus before men, then one day he will be ashamed of us before his Father and the angels.

Fifthly, *how precious a grace is faith.* Jesus 'said to her, "Daughter, your faith has made you well; go in peace, and be healed of your disease."'

Of all the Christian graces, none is so frequently mentioned in the New Testament as faith, and none is so highly commended. *No grace brings such glory to Christ.* Hope brings an eager expectation of good things to come. Love brings a warm and willing heart. Faith brings an empty hand, receives everything, and can give nothing in return. *No grace is so important to the Christian's own soul.* By faith we begin, live and stand. We walk by faith and not by sight. By faith we overcome. By faith we have peace, and enter into rest. *No grace should be the subject of so much self-inquiry.* We should often ask ourselves, Do I really believe? Is my faith true, genuine, and the gift of God? Let a sinner only 'touch' Jesus, and he will be made whole.

5:35–43

A great miracle is recorded in these verses: a dead girl is restored to life. Mighty as the 'king of terrors' is, there is one mightier than he. The keys of death are in our Lord's hands. The day will come when 'He will swallow up death for ever' (Isaiah 25:8).

Learn firstly, that *rank places no man beyond the reach of sorrow.* Jairus was 'one of the rulers of the synagogue', yet sickness and trouble came to his house. It is well for us all to remember this. We often think and talk as if the possession of rank or riches was the great antidote to sorrow or that it could secure us against sickness and death. It is the very extreme of blindness to think so. Death comes everywhere and to everyone. It does not stand on any ceremony. We are told that 'it is appointed for man to die once, and after that comes judgment' (Hebrews 9:27). All are going to one place—the grave. Happy are those who set their affections on heaven, for they, and they only, have a treasure which is incorruptible.

Secondly, *how almighty is the power of our Lord Jesus Christ.* That message which pierced Jairus' heart, telling him that his child was dead, did not stop Jesus for a moment. At once he cheered the father's fainting spirits with these gracious words: 'Do not fear, only believe.' Jesus came to the house, where he found 'people weeping and wailing loudly'. He entered the room where the daughter was lying, took her by the hand, and said, 'Little girl, I say to you, arise.' At once her heart began to beat again and breath returned to her lifeless body. 'And immediately the girl got up and began walking.' No wonder 'they were immediately overcome with amazement'.

Think for a moment how wonderful was the change which took place in that house. From weeping to rejoicing, from mourning to delight, from death to life. There must have been a happy family gathering that night!

See in this glorious miracle a proof of what Jesus can do for dead souls. He can raise our children from the death of trespasses and sins, and make them walk before him in newness of life. He can take our sons and daughters by the hand, and say to them, 'arise', and bid them live not to themselves, but to him who died for them and rose again. Have we a dead soul in our family? Let us send to Jesus message after message, and plead with him to help. He that came to the aid of Jairus is still plenteous in mercy and mighty in power.

Finally, see in this miracle *a blessed pledge of what our Lord will do in the day of his second appearing*. He will call his believing people from their graves. He will give them a better, more glorious, and more beautiful body than they had in the days of their pilgrimage here on the earth. He will gather together his elect from north, south, east and west, to part no more and to die no more. Believing parents shall once more see believing children, and believing husbands shall once more see believing wives. Let us 'not grieve as others do who have no hope' (1 Thessalonians 4:13) over those who fall asleep in Christ. Let us look forward. There is a glorious resurrection morning yet to come.

Chapter 6

6:1–6

This passage shows us our Lord Jesus Christ in 'his hometown', at Nazareth. It is a melancholy illustration of the wickedness of man's heart, and deserves special attention.

First of all, we see *how apt men are to undervalue things with which they are familiar*. Many at Nazareth 'took offence at him'. They could not think it possible that one who had lived so many years among themselves, and whose brothers and sisters they knew, could deserve to be followed as a public teacher.

No place on earth ever had such privileges as Nazareth. For thirty years the Son of God lived there. For all that time he walked with God before their eyes, living a blameless, perfect life. But it was all lost on them. They were not ready to believe the gospel when the Lord came among them and taught in their synagogue. They refused to acknowledge that he had any right to claim their attention.

There is nothing to surprise us here. The same thing is going on around us every day in our own land. The holy Scriptures, the preaching of the gospel, the public ordinances of religion, the abundant means of grace that as a nation we enjoy, are continually undervalued among us. As so often, familiarity breeds contempt.

There is comfort in this part of our Lord's experience for some of the Lord's people—comfort for faithful ministers of the gospel, who are cast down by the unbelief of so many, even among their hearers—comfort for true Christians who stand alone in their families, and see all those around them cleaving to the world. They are drinking the same cup as their beloved Master. He too was despised most by those who knew him best. Let them know that the sorrowful words of their Lord will generally be fulfilled in the experience of his servants, 'A prophet is not without honour, except in his hometown and among his relatives and in his own household.'

Secondly, we see *how humble was the rank of life which our Lord condescended to occupy before he began his public ministry*. The people of Nazareth said of him in contempt, 'Is not this the carpenter?' This expression is only found in Mark's Gospel. It shows plainly that while living at Nazareth, Jesus was not ashamed to work with his own hands. There is something marvellous in this thought! He who made heaven and earth, the sea, and everything in it—He, without whom 'was not anything made that was made' (John 1:3)—the Son of God himself, took on himself the form of servant, and lived as a working man. This is indeed 'the love of Christ that surpasses knowledge' (Ephesians 3:19)—'that though he was rich, yet for (our) sake he became poor' (2 Corinthians 8:9).

The thought of the carpenter's shop at Nazareth should cast down the high thoughts of all who make an idol of riches. It cannot be dishonourable to occupy the same position as the Son of God and Saviour of the world. Both in life and death he humbled himself, that through him sinners might live and reign for evermore.

Finally, we see *how exceedingly sinful is the sin of unbelief*. Two remarkable expressions are used in teaching this lesson. One is, that our Lord 'could do no mighty work' at Nazareth, by reason of the hardness of the people's hearts. The other is, that 'he marvelled because of their unbelief'. The one shows that unbelief has the power to rob people of the highest blessings. The other shows that it is so suicidal and unreasonable a sin that even the Son of God regards it with surprise.

We can never be too much on our guard against unbelief. It is the oldest sin in the world, having begun in the garden of Eden, when Eve listened to the devil's promises instead of believing God's words. It is the most ruinous of all sins in its consequences, as well as being the most foolish and inconsistent of them. It is the commonest sin in the world, making a man refuse the plainest evidence, shut his eyes against the clearest testimony, and yet believe lies.

Let us watch our own hearts carefully in the matter of unbelief, and go on doing the same even after we have believed. The root of unbelief is never entirely destroyed. We have only to leave aside watching and praying, and a crop of unbelief will soon spring up. The humble, child-like heart is the heart that believes. No prayer is so important as that of the disciples in their urgent request to Jesus, 'Increase our faith!' (Luke 17:5).

A note is needed on the expression that Jesus 'could do no mighty work there ... because of their unbelief'. This cannot mean that it was impossible for him to do a mighty work there, or that although he had the will to do mighty works, he was prevented by a power greater than his own. Such a view would be dishonouring to our Lord, and would amount to a practical denial of his deity. With Jesus, nothing is impossible. If he had willed to do mighty works, without question he had the power.

The meaning must be that he *would* not do any mighty work there, because of the unbelief that he saw. He perceived the state of the people's hearts, and would not waste signs and wonders on an unbelieving and hardened generation.

6:7–13

These verses describe the first sending forth of the apostles to preach. The great head of the church made proof of his ministers, before he left them alone in the world. He trained them for the work they were one day to do, when finally left to themselves. Well would it be for the church if all ministers of the gospel were prepared for duty in like manner, and did not so often take up their office untried, unproved and inexperienced.

Observe here *how our Lord Jesus Christ sent out his apostles 'two by two'*. Mark is the only evangelist who mentions this fact, and it deserves special notice. Without doubt, it is intended to teach us the advantages of Christian company to all who work for Christ. 'Two are better than one' (Ecclesiastes 4:9). Two will help one another in judgment, aid one another in difficulties, stir one another up when tempted to idleness, and comfort one another in times of trial.

One thing is clear, and that is the duty of all who serve Christ to work together and help one another whenever they can. 'Iron sharpens iron, and one man sharpens another' (Proverbs 27:17). The words of Hebrews 10:24-25 must not be forgotten: 'And let us consider how to stir up one another to love and good works, not neglecting to meet together, as is the habit of some.'

Secondly, observe *what solemn words Jesus uses about those who will not receive or hear his ministers*. He says, 'if any place will not receive you and they will not listen to you, when you leave, shake off the dust that is on your feet as a testimony against them'.

One of the greatest sins anyone can commit in the sight of God is to hear the gospel of Christ and not believe it—to be called upon to repent and believe, and yet to remain careless and unbelieving. So let us ask ourselves: what are we doing with the gospel? Have we received it into our hearts? Have we really obeyed it in our lives?

Lastly, observe *what the doctrine was which our Lord's apostles preached*. 'So they went out and proclaimed that people should repent.'

The necessity of repentance may seem at first sight a very simple and elementary truth. Yet it is inseparably connected with right views of God, human nature, sin, Christ, holiness and heaven. Romans 3:23 declares, 'for all have sinned and fall short of the glory of God'. All need to be brought to a sense of their sins, to a sorrow for them, to a willingness to give them up, and to a hunger and thirst after pardon. All need to be born again and to flee to Christ. This is 'repentance that leads to life' (Acts 11:18). Nothing less than this is required for the salvation of any sinner.

Have we ourselves repented? It is well to know that the apostles taught it, but it is far better to know repentance by experience and to feel it inwardly in our own hearts. There are no impenitent people in the kingdom of heaven.

6:14–29

These verses describe the death of one of the most eminent saints of God. They record the murder of John the Baptist. Let us see what practical lessons the passage contains for our own souls.

We see, firstly, *the amazing power of truth over the conscience*. Herod fears John while he lives and is troubled about him after he dies. A friendless, solitary preacher, with no other weapon than God's truth, disturbs and terrifies a king.

Everyone has a conscience. This is why Felix 'was alarmed' (Acts 24:25) and Agrippa said 'would you persuade me to become a Christian?' (Acts 25:28), when Paul the prisoner spoke before them. God has not left himself without witness in the hearts of unconverted people. Fallen and corrupt as man is, there are thoughts within him accusing or excusing, according as how he lives.

We see, secondly, *how far people may go in religion, and yet miss salvation by yielding to one master sin*. Herod went further than many. He 'feared John, knowing that he was a righteous and holy man, and he kept him safe. When he heard him, he was greatly perplexed, and yet he heard him gladly'. But there was one thing which Herod would not do. He would not cease from adultery. He would not give up Herodias. And so he ruined his soul for ever.

Let us take warning from Herod's case. Let us keep back nothing that stands between us and salvation. Let us often look within, and make sure that there is no darling lust or pet transgression which, Herodias-like, is murdering our souls. Let us not rest until we can say with the psalmist, 'Therefore I consider all your precepts to be right; I hate every false way' (Psalm 119:128).

We see, thirdly, *how boldly a faithful minister of God ought to rebuke sin*. John spoke plainly to Herod about the wickedness of his life. He did not excuse himself under the plea that it was impudent, impolitic, untimely or useless to speak out. He did not say smooth things or use soft words. He told his royal hearer the plain truth, regardless of all consequences: 'It is not lawful for you to have your brother's wife.'

Here is a pattern for all ministers to follow. Publicly and privately, from the pulpit and in private visits, they ought to rebuke all open sin and deliver a faithful warning to all who are living in it. It may give offence and bring great unpopularity. With all this they have nothing to do. Duties are theirs, results are God's.

No doubt it requires great grace and courage to do this, and such work must be gone about wisely and lovingly. But it is a matter in which a Christian minister's character for faithfulness and love are at stake. If he believes someone is injuring their soul, he ought surely to tell them. If he loves them truly and tenderly, he ought not to let them ruin themselves unwarned. 'Whoever rebukes a man will afterward find more favour than he who flatters with his tongue' (Proverbs 28:23).

We see, fourthly, *how bitterly people hate a reprover, when they are determined to keep their sins*. Herodias, the king's unhappy partner in iniquity, seems to have sunk even deeper in sin than Herod. Hardened and seared in conscience by her wickedness, she hated John for his faithful testimony, and never rested until she had procured his death.

We need not wonder at this. When men and women have chosen their course, and resolved to have things their own wicked way, they dislike anyone who tries to turn them. They wish to be left alone, are irritated by opposition, and angry when told the truth. So let it never surprise us when we hear of faithful ministers of the gospel (and Christians as a whole) being spoken against, hated and reviled. It is no disgrace to be disliked by the wicked and the ungodly. Those words of our Lord are not enough considered: 'Woe to you, when all people speak well of you' (Luke 6:26).

We see, fifthly, *how much sin may sometimes follow from feasting and revelling*. Herod kept his birthday with a splendid banquet, and, in a moment of excitement, granted a wicked girl's request to have the head of John the Baptist cut off. Even if he regretted it bitterly the next day, the deed was done and it was too late.

This is a faithful picture of what can easily result from feasting and merry-making. People do things at such times from heated feelings, which afterwards they deeply regret, and even repent of. Happy are those who keep clear of temptations and avoid giving occasion to the devil. No one knows what they might end up doing once they venture off safe ground.

We see, finally, *how little reward some of God's best servants receive in this world*. An unjust imprisonment and a violent death were the last fruit that John reaped in return for his labour. He was called to seal his testimony with his blood.

Histories like this are intended to remind us that the true Christian's best things are yet to come. His rest, his crown, his wages, his reward are all on the other side of the grave. Here, in this world, he must walk by faith, and not by sight. If he looks for the praise of man, he will be disappointed. Here, in this life, he must sow and labour, fight and endure persecution. If he expects an earthly reward, he expects what he will not find. But this life is not all. There is to be a day of reckoning. There is a glorious harvest yet to come. Heaven will make amends for all. 'For I consider that the sufferings of this present time are not worth comparing with the glory that is to be revealed to us' (Romans 8:18). 'For this slight momentary affliction is preparing for us an eternal weight of glory beyond all comparison' (2 Corinthians 4:17).

6:30–34

Three lessons, in particular, await us here. First of all, note *the conduct of the apostles when they returned from their first mission as preachers.* We learn that they 'returned to Jesus and told him all that they had done and taught'. We should follow their example, and do daily what the apostles did on this occasion. How important it is to spread all our work before Christ, seeking from him counsel, guidance, strength and help.

Prayer is the main secret of success in spiritual business. It moves God who can move heaven and earth, and brings down the promised aid of the Holy Spirit, without whom all is in vain. It is not always those who have the most eminent gifts who are the most successful labourers for God. It is generally those who keep up closest communion with Christ and are most instant in prayer.

Note, secondly, *the words of Jesus to the apostles when they returned from their first public ministry.* 'And he said to them, "Come away by yourselves to a desolate place and rest a while."' Our Lord shows tender consideration here, knowing well that his servants are flesh as well as spirit, and have bodies as well as souls. He knows that, at best, they have a treasure in earthen vessels and are compassed with many infirmities.

As well as tender consideration, Jesus' words show deep wisdom. He knows well that his servants must attend to their own souls as well as the souls of others. He knows that a constant attention to public work is apt to make us forget our own soul-business. So we must never cease to watch our own hearts closely, and make time for regular self-examination and calm meditation.

Note, finally, *the feelings of Jesus towards the people who came together to him.* We are told that 'he had compassion on them, because they were like sheep without a shepherd'. They had no teachers or guides, and no spiritual food. Thousands of immortal souls were there before our Lord, ignorant, helpless and on the high road to ruin. This touched the gracious heart of Jesus, so 'he began to teach them many things'.

Let us never forget that our Lord 'Jesus Christ is the same yesterday and today and forever' (Hebrews 13:8). He never changes. High in heaven, at God's right hand, he still looks with compassion on the children of men. Special as his love is towards his own sheep who hear his voice, he still has a love of real pity and compassion for everyone. Still he cares for people's souls, is willing to save them, and invites them to believe upon him and be saved.

As we leave this passage, let us ask ourselves whether we know anything of the mind of Christ. Are we, like him, tenderly concerned about the souls of the unconverted? Do we, like him, fell compassion for all who are still sheep who have no shepherd? Are we concerned for those near our doors, as well as for those in foreign lands, and for the spread of the gospel in every place? The person who cares nothing for the souls of other people is not like Jesus.

6:35–46

Of all Jesus' miracles, none is so frequently described in the Gospels as the one in this present passage, for each of the four evangelists (Matthew, Mark, Luke and John) was inspired to record it.

Observe, for one thing, *what an example this miracle affords of our Lord Jesus Christ's almighty power*. We are told that he fed 'five thousand men' with 'five loaves' and 'two fish'. That is all the food that was there. Yet we read that Jesus took these few loaves and fish, blessed them, 'and gave them to the disciples to set before the people'. We are then told that 'they all ate and were satisfied'—and that there were then 'twelve baskets full of broken pieces and of the fish' that were gathered up. Here was creative power belonging only to God—he who made the world out of nothing.

As Christians, we live in the midst of an evil world, seeing few with us and many against us. Our hearts are often weak, and the devil is continually busy seeking to bring us to a stop. Where shall we turn for comfort? What shall keep faith alive and preserve us from sinking in despair? There is only one answer. We must look to Jesus, thinking on his almighty power and his wonders of old time, and recalling an occasion like this one when he created so much food for so many people. He still lives, he never changes, and he is on our side.

Observe, for another thing, *our Lord Jesus Christ's conduct when the miracle of feeding the multitude had been performed*. 'After he had taken leave of them, he went up on the mountain to pray.'

He did not seek the praise of men. After one of his greatest miracles, we find him immediately seeking solitude, and spending his time in prayer. No one ever did such mighty works as he did. No one ever spoke such words as he spoke. No one was ever so urgent in prayer. So let Jesus' conduct in this respect be our example. We cannot work miracles, but we can walk in his steps in the matter of private devotion. He teaches us, 'when you pray, go into your room and shut the door and pray to your Father who is in secret' (Matthew 6:6). Let us strive to make time, place and opportunity for being alone with God. Above all, let us not only pray before we attempt to work for God, but pray also after our work is done.

There is much room for self-examination here. Within the twenty-four hours of the day, what time do we give to prayer? What progress can we mark, from year to year, in the fervency and fullness of our praying? These are humbling inquiries, but they are useful for our souls. There are few things, it may be feared, in which Christians come so far short of Christ's example, as they do in the matter of prayer. Let us seek to imitate Jesus' life of prayer, and not merely talk of it or admire it.

6:47–56

The event recorded first in these verses is a beautiful emblem of the position of all believers between the first and second comings of Jesus Christ. Like the disciples, we are now tossed to and fro by storms, and do not enjoy the visible presence of our Lord. Like the disciples, we shall see our Lord face to face again. Like the disciples, we shall see all things changed for the better, when our Master comes to us.

There is nothing fanciful in such an application of the passage. For the present, however, let us confine ourselves to the plain, practical lessons contained here.

Notice, in the first place, *how our Lord sees the troubles of his believing people, and in due time will help them.* When 'the boat was out on the sea, and he was alone on the land', Jesus saw that his disciples 'were making headway painfully'—he came to them 'walking on the sea'—he cheered them with the gracious words, 'Take heart; it is I. Do not be afraid'—and he changed the storm into a calm.

There are thoughts of comfort here for all true believers. Wherever they may be, or however their circumstances may be, the Lord Jesus sees them. We are never beyond the reach of his care. Our way is never hid from him. He 'knows the way that (we) take' (Job 23:10), and is still able to help. He may not come to our aid at the time we like best, but he will never allow us utterly to fail. He who walked upon the water never changes. He will always come at the right time to uphold his people. Jesus sees us, and will not forsake us.

Notice, in the second place, *the fears of the disciples when they first saw Jesus walking on the sea.* We are told that 'when they saw him walking on the sea they thought it was a ghost, and cried out, for they all saw him and were terrified'.

What a faithful picture of human nature we have in these words. How many, if they had seen what the disciples saw, would have behaved in the same manner! How few, in similar circumstances, would preserve their composure and be altogether free from fears! The truth is, there is an instinctive feeling in everyone which makes them shrink from anything which seems to belong to another world. However, every true Christian's clear duty is to live provided with an antidote against all fears of the great unseen world. That antidote is faith in an unseen Saviour, and constant fellowship with him. So armed, and 'seeing him who is invisible' (Hebrews 11:27), nothing need make us afraid. With Jesus for our shepherd, we have no cause for alarm. With Jesus as our shield, we are safe.

Notice, in conclusion, *what a bright example we have of our duty to one another.* We learn that when 'they came to land at Gennesaret and moored to the shore', Jesus was immediately recognised, with the result that folk 'ran about the whole region and began to bring the sick people on their beds to wherever they heard he was'. As a result, 'wherever he came, in villages, cities, or countryside, they laid the sick in the marketplaces and implored him that they might touch even the fringe of his garment'.

There is a pattern here for us. Let us 'go, and do likewise' (Luke 10:37). Let us seek to bring all around us who are in need of spiritual medicine to Jesus, the great physician, that they may be healed. Souls are dying every day. Time is short. Opportunities are rapidly passing away. As Jesus himself declared, 'night is coming, when no one can work' (John 9:4). Let us spare no pains in labouring to bring men and women to the knowledge of Jesus Christ, that they may be saved. It is a comfortable thought, that 'as many as touched (him) were made well'.

Chapter 7

7:1–13

This passage contains a humbling picture of what human nature is capable of doing in religion. It is one of those Scriptures which ought to be studied frequently and carefully by all who desire the prosperity of Christ's church.

The first thing demanding our attention is *the low and degraded condition of Jewish religion when our Lord was upon earth*. We find the principal teachers of the Jewish nation finding fault because 'some of his [Jesus'] disciples ate with hands that were defiled, that is, unwashed'. We are told that they attached great importance to 'the washing of cups and pots and copper vessels and dining couches'. In short, the man who paid most rigid attention to mere external observances of human invention was reckoned the holiest man!

Remember that the nation in which this state of things existed was the most highly favoured in the world. To it was given the law on Mount Sinai, the service of God, the priesthood, the covenants and the promises. Moses, Samuel, David and the prophets lived and died among its people. No nation on earth ever had so many spiritual privileges—yet no nation ever misused its privileges so fearfully, and so thoroughly forsook its own mercies. Never did fine gold become so dim! No wonder that in the time of Jesus' earthly ministry, he found the people like sheep without a shepherd. External observances alone feed no consciences and sanctify no hearts.

Let all of this be a warning to us never to trifle with false doctrine. Once leave the King's highway of truth, and we may end with washing cups and pots like the Pharisees and scribes. There are parts of the Christian church today in which the Scriptures are scarcely read and the gospel never preached—parts in which the only religion now remaining consists in using a few unmeaning forms and keeping certain man-made fasts and feasts. Let us contend earnestly 'for the faith that was once for all delivered to the saints' (Jude 3).

The second thing demanding our attention is *the uselessness of mere lip-service in the worship of God.* Jesus enforces this lesson with a quotation from the Old Testament: 'Well did Isaiah prophesy of you hypocrites, as it is written, "This people honours me with their lips, but their heart is far from me."'

The heart is that part of man which God chiefly notices. The bowed head and the bended knee, the grave face and the rigid posture—all these together do not make a spiritual worshipper. He requires the worship of the heart, and says to every one of us, 'give me your heart' (Proverbs 23:26).

Let us remember this in both the public congregation and our private devotions. Regarding the former, we must not be content to take our bodies to church and leave our hearts at home. Whatever those who see us think, it is all worse than nothing in God's sight, if our hearts are far away. Regarding the latter, we must not be satisfied saying good words, if our imaginations are roving far away at the same time. It profits us nothing at all. Heart-prayers are the prayers he loves to hear, and are the only prayers he will answer. Though we may feel our petitions are weak and stammering, yet, if they come from a right heart, God understands them. Such prayers are his delight.

The last thing demanding our attention is *the tendency of man's inventions in religion to supplant God's word.* Three times we find this charge brought forward by Jesus against the Pharisees: 'You leave the commandment of God and hold to the tradition of men', 'You have a fine way of rejecting the commandment of God in order to establish your tradition', and 'making void the word of God by your tradition that you have handed down'. Their first step was to add their traditions to the Scriptures. The second was to place those traditions of their own on a level with the word of God, and give them equal authority. The last was to honour them above the Scriptures, and so to degrade Scripture from its lawful position.

It is a mournful fact that Christians have far too often walked in the steps of the Pharisees in this matter. Religious observances of man's invention have been pressed on Christians for their acceptance. These have in due course been urged with more vigour than God's own commandments, and defended with more zeal than the authority of God's own word.

Let us be careful of attempting to add anything to the word of God as necessary to salvation. It provokes God. It is as good as saying that his Bible is not perfect, and that we know better than he does. The whole Bible, and nothing but the Bible, must be our rule of faith—nothing added and nothing taken away. What God requires is essential to life eternal. Whoever disobeys it ruins his own soul.

Before leaving this passage, notice, from the example Jesus gives, the subtle way in which the Pharisees sought to evade the requirements of the fifth commandment ('Honour your father and your mother', Exodus 20:12). They did not openly deny that obligation, yet they contrived to make it void. What they did was this. They taught that a man might dedicate to God's service, as sacred, any part of his property which might be applied to his parents' relief, and so discharge himself of any further expense about them. A person only had to say, 'What you would have gained from me is Corban, (that is, given to God)', and no further claim could be made upon him for his father's or mother's support. Under the pretence of giving God a prior claim, he set himself free from the burden of maintaining them for ever.

7:14–23

To begin with, we see here *how slow in understanding men are in spiritual things*. Jesus says to the people, 'Hear me, all of you, and understand.' 'Then are you also without understanding?' He says to the disciples, 'Do you not see…?'

The corruption of human nature is a universal disease. It affects not only a person's heart, will and conscience, but their mind, memory and understanding as well. The very same person who is quick and clever in worldly things will often utterly fail to comprehend the simplest truths of Christianity. He will often be unable to take in the plainest reasonings of the gospel, and will see no meaning in the clearest statements of evangelical doctrine. For 'the world did not know God through wisdom' (1 Corinthians 1:21).

We must pray daily for the teaching of the Holy Spirit, if we would make progress in the knowledge of divine things. Without him, the mightiest intellect and the strongest reasoning powers will not carry us far. A humble, teachable, childlike frame of mind is the grand secret of success. Happy is the one who often says with the psalmist, 'teach me your statutes' (Psalm 119:64). Such a one will understand as well as hear.

Secondly, we see *that the heart is the chief source of defilement and impurity in God's sight.* Moral purity does not depend on washing or not washing, touching things or not touching them, eating things or not eating them, as the scribes and Pharisees taught. What defiles us, Jesus teaches here, is not what 'goes into a person from outside', but those things which come 'from within, out of the heart of man'.

Our original sinfulness and natural inclination to evil are all too often overlooked. They are ascribed to bad examples, bad company, particular temptations or the snares of the devil. It seems forgotten that everyone carries within themselves a fountain of wickedness. We need no bad company to teach us to sin, and no devil to tempt us, in order to run into sin. We have within us the beginning of every sin under heaven. We ought to remember this in the training and education of children. The seeds of all mischief and wickedness are in their hearts, and parents must be diligent in praying for their children's conversion.

Finally, we see *what a black catalogue of evils the human heart contains.* Jesus declares, 'for from within, out of the heart of man, come evil thoughts, sexual immorality, theft, murder, adultery, coveting, wickedness, deceit, sensuality, envy, slander, pride, foolishness. All these evil things come from within, and they defile a person'.

It is very important to understand that, in saying this, Jesus is speaking of the human heart generally, all mankind, and not only, for example, only of criminals in prison. All of us have by nature such a heart as Jesus here describes. The seeds of all these evils lie hidden within us all. They may lie dormant, or be restrained by fear of consequences or the dread of discovery—and, above all, by the almighty grace of God. But the root of every sin is within us all.

How humble we ought to be, when we read these verses, for God reads our hearts. How thankful we ought to be for the gospel, when we read them, for the blood of Christ can cleanse us and the Holy Spirit change us. And how watchful we ought to be, when we read them, and what a careful guard we need to keep continually upon our imaginations, tongues and daily behaviour.

7:24–30

We know nothing of the woman mentioned here, beyond the facts set before us. Her name, her former history, the way in which she (a Gentile, living in 'the region of Tyre and Sidon') was led to seek the Lord—all these things are kept from us. Yet the few facts that are related concerning her are full of precious instruction.

In the first place, *this passage is meant to encourage us to pray for others*. The woman must have been in deep affliction. Her 'little daughter was possessed by an unclean spirit'. Hearing of Jesus, she 'came and fell down at his feet' and 'begged him to cast the demon out of her daughter'. She prayed for one who could not pray for herself, and would not rest until her prayer was granted. By prayer she obtained the cure which no human means could obtain. Hopeless and desperate though the girl's case appeared, she had a praying mother, and where there is a praying mother there is always hope.

The truth taught here is one of deep importance. The case recorded here is one that does not stand alone. Few duties are so strongly recommended by Scriptural example as the duty of intercessory prayer. The nobleman's son at Capernaum, the centurion's servant and Jairus' daughter are all striking examples. Wonderful as it may seem, God is pleased to do great things for souls, when friends and relatives are moved to pray for them. In particular, the prayers of fathers and mothers are heard on high. Parents cannot give their children new hearts, a mind to love God, or a will to choose Christ's service. Yet there is one thing they can always do—they can pray for them. Even when the sons and daughters will not allow their parents to speak to them of Christ and the gospel, they cannot prevent us speaking to God for them.

In the second place, *this passage is meant to teach us to persevere in praying for others.* The woman before us here appeared at first to obtain nothing by her application to the Lord. Indeed, Jesus' reply was discouraging. Yet she did not give up in despair. She prayed on, and did not faint, taking no refusal. She pleaded for a few 'crumbs' of mercy, rather than none at all. And she was granted success in her praying. She heard at last Jesus say to her these joyful words: 'For this statement you may go your way; the demon has left your daughter.'

Perseverance in prayer is a great matter. Our hearts are all too apt to become cool and indifferent, and to think that it is no use to draw near to God—particularly when we see no immediate answer to our prayers, especially for people's conversions. So, in order to arm our minds with arguments for pressing on in intercessory prayer, let us often study the case of this woman. Let us remember that, although she faced great discouragement to begin with, she kept on—and at last she went home rejoicing. Let us resolve, by God's grace, to follow her example. Let us beware of selfish prayers—prayers which are taken up wholly with our own affairs. Let us name all whom we love before God continually. And let us pray for all, even the most unbelieving, in spite of their continuing unbelief, and even if God's time of mercy for them may yet be a distant one.

7:31–37

Three lessons stand out for us in these verses. First of all, note *the mighty miracle that is here recorded.* We read that 'they brought to (Jesus) a man who was deaf and had a speech impediment, and they begged him to lay his hand on him'. At once the petition was granted and the man was cured. 'And his ears were opened, his tongue was released, and he spoke plainly.'

There is more here, however, than only an example of our Lord's power, remarkable though that is. For, looking more deeply into what happened, we are intended to see his power to heal the spiritually deaf. He can give the chief of sinners a hearing ear, so that he delights in listening to the very gospel which he once ridiculed and despised. And we see also Jesus' power to heal the spiritually dumb. He can teach the hardest of transgressors to call upon God, and can put a new song into the mouth of one whose talk was once only of this world. He can make the vilest of men speak of spiritual things, and testify to the gospel of the grace of God. When Jesus pours forth his Spirit, nothing is impossible.

Note, secondly, *the peculiar manner in which our Lord thought it good to work the miracle here recorded.* The man being brought to Jesus, we are told that 'taking him aside from the crowd privately, he put his fingers into his ears, and after spitting touched his tongue'. Then, 'looking up to heaven, he sighed and said to him, "Ephphatha", that is "Be opened."'

There is much that is mysterious in these actions, but there is one simple lesson to be learned from Jesus's conduct here: he was not tied to the use of any one means in doing his works among men. Sometimes he thought fit to work in one way, sometimes in another. And we see the same thing going on in his church today. In conveying grace to the soul, sometimes Jesus is pleased to work by the word preached publicly, sometimes by the word read privately. Sometimes he awakens souls by sickness and affliction, sometimes by the rebukes or counsel of friends. His providences are many and varied. All his ways of working are in turn employed for the same great end, the conversion of souls. All are in the hands of him who knows best which to use in each separate case with which he deals.

Note, finally, *the remarkable testimony which was borne by those who saw the miracle here recorded.* They said of our Lord, 'He has done all things well.' Maybe those who said these words little knew their full meaning when applied to Christ. But the truth to which they gave utterance is full of deep and unspeakable comfort, and ought daily to be remembered by all true Christians.

Let us remember it as we look back over the past days of our lives, from when we were converted. Jesus has always 'done all things well'. In first bringing us out of darkness into marvellous light—in humbling us and teaching us our weakness, guilt and folly—in stripping us of our idols and choosing all our circumstances—in placing us where we are and giving us what we have—how well everything has been done! How great the mercy that we have not had our own way!

Let us remember it as we look forward to the days yet to come. We do not know what they may be—bright or dark, many or few. But we know that we are in the hands of him who does 'all things well'. He will not err in any of his dealings with us. He will take away and give—afflict and bereave—move us and settle us, with perfect wisdom, at the right time, in the right way. The great Shepherd of the sheep makes no mistakes. He leads every lamb of his flock by the right way to the city of habitation.

We shall never see the full beauty of these words until the resurrection morning. We shall then look back over our lives, and know the meaning of everything that happened from first to last. We shall remember all the way by which we were led, and confess that all was well done. The whys and wherefores, the causes and reasons of everything which now perplexes, will be clear and plain as the sun at noon-day. We shall wonder at our own blindness, and marvel that we could ever have doubted our Lord's love.

Chapter 8

8:1–13

Once more we see Jesus feeding a great multitude with a few loaves and fishes. He knew the heart of man, and that many would question the reality of the wonderful works he performed. So now—publicly and before some four thousand witnesses—he shows his almighty power a second time.

Observe first, *how great is the kindness and compassion of our Lord Jesus Christ*. He saw around him 'a great crowd' who 'had nothing to eat'. He knew that many were following him out of idle curiosity, and had no claim to be regarded as his disciples. Yet when he saw them hungry and needy, he took pity on them: 'I have compassion on the crowd, because they have been with me now three days and have nothing to eat.'

The feeling heart of Jesus appears in these words. He has compassion even on those who are not his people—the faithless, the graceless, the followers of this world. He feels tenderly for them, though they do not realise it. He died for such, though they care little about him. He would receive them graciously, and pardon them freely, if they would only repent of their sin and believe on him. Let us beware of measuring the love of Christ by human measures.

We must strive to make Jesus our pattern in this, as well as in everything else. Let us be kind, compassionate and courteous to all people. We should seek to 'do good to everyone', and not only 'to those who are of the household of faith' (Galatians 6:10). This is to show the mind of Christ.

Observe next, *that with Christ nothing is impossible*. The disciples asked, 'How can one feed these people with bread here in this desolate place?' They might well say so, for without the hand of him who first made the world out of nothing, the thing could not be. Yet in the almighty hands of Jesus, 'seven loaves' and 'a few small fish' were made sufficient to satisfy 'about four thousand people'. Nothing is too hard for the Lord.

We must never allow ourselves to doubt Christ's power to supply the spiritual needs of all his people. He has ample for every soul that trusts in him. Though we are conscious of how weak, corrupt and empty we feel, let us never despair. For in Jesus there resides a boundless store of mercy and grace, ready to be bestowed on all who ask in prayer.

And let us never doubt, either, Christ's providential care for the temporal needs of his people. He knows our circumstances and is acquainted with all our necessities. His heart is not changed since he ascended up on high and sat down on the right hand of God. Our faith may sometimes be tried. We may on occasions be kept waiting and be brought very low. But the believer will never be left entirely in extremity.

Observe finally, *how much sorrow unbelief occasions to our Lord Jesus Christ*. 'The Pharisees came and began to argue with him, seeking from him a sign from heaven to test him. And he sighed deeply in his spirit.' That sigh came from a heart mourning over the ruin that these wicked men were bringing on their own souls. Enemies though they were, Jesus could not behold them hardening themselves in unbelief without sorrow.

The feeling Jesus expresses here will always be the feeling of all true Christians. Grief over the sins of others is one leading evidence of true grace. Whoever is truly converted will always regard the unconverted with pity and concern. So, do we know anything of likeness to Christ and fellow-feeling with him? Do we feel pained and sorrowful when we see people continuing in sin and unbelief? Do we feel grieved and concerned over the state of the unconverted?

8:14–21

Two lessons stand out in these verses. Notice, firstly, *the solemn warning our Lord gives to his disciples*. 'Watch out; beware of the leaven of the Pharisees and the leaven of Herod.' By 'leaven', Jesus meant not the leaven of bread but the leaven of doctrine. The objects of his caution were the self-righteousness and formalism of the Pharisees, and the worldliness and scepticism of Herod and his court. Against both, Jesus bids his disciples to be on their guard.

Such warnings are of deep importance, and the church of Christ needs always to remember them. The assaults of persecution from outside have never done half so much harm to the church as the rise of false doctrines within. Indeed, the matters Jesus specifies here—formalism on the one hand and scepticism on the other—have always been found to inflict most injury on the cause of Christianity. They are chronic diseases, and in every age multitudes of Christians have been infected by them.

The word 'leaven' that Jesus uses is very appropriate. It describes exactly the small beginnings of false doctrine, the subtle quiet way in which it pervades the truth, and the deadly power with which it alters the whole character of Christianity. That charge is needful which reads: 'Examine yourselves, to see whether you are in the faith. Test yourselves' (2 Corinthians 13:5), and 'beware' of leaven. 'A little leaven leavens the whole lump' (Galatians 5:9).

Notice, secondly, *the dull understanding of the disciples*, when Jesus gave them this warning. They thought that he was talking to them about bread. It never struck them that he was speaking about doctrine. As a result, they drew from him this sharp reproof: 'Do you not yet perceive or understand? Are your hearts hardened?' Believers though these disciples were, they were still dull of apprehension in spiritual things. Their eyes were still dim, and their perception slow in the matters of the kingdom of God.

Discovering this may help to correct the high thoughts we are apt to entertain of our own wisdom, and to keep us humble and lowly-minded. We do not know everything the moment we are converted. Our knowledge, like all our graces, is always imperfect, and there is always more ignorance in our hearts than we are aware of. 'If anyone imagines that he knows something, he does not yet know as he ought to know' (1 Corinthians 8:2). So let us remember this, especially when dealing with young Christians—bearing with them patiently, giving them time to grow in grace and knowledge, never despising their weakness or dullness.

8:22–26

We do not know the reason for the particular means employed by our Lord Jesus Christ, in working the miracle recorded in these verses. They narrate the miraculous healing of 'a blind man'. Yet rather than healing him with just a word or a touch, Jesus 'took the blind man by the hand and led him out of the village'. Then, not until Jesus had spat 'on his eyes and laid his hands on him', was the man's sight restored.

In this, we learn (once again) that the Lord is not tied to the use of any one means in all that he does. In the conversion of men's souls, for example, there are varieties of operation, but it is always the Holy Spirit who converts. So it is with the healing of bodies—there were varieties of agency employed by Jesus, but it was always the same divine power that effected the cure.

Particularly noteworthy in this passage is the gradual nature of the cure. Jesus did not deliver him from his blindness at once, but by degrees. He might have done it in a moment, but he chose to do it step by step. At first, the man said, 'I see men, but they look like trees, walking.' Afterwards, when his eyesight was restored completely, 'he saw everything clearly'. In this respect, this miracle stands entirely alone.

We need hardly doubt that this gradual cure was intended to be an emblem of spiritual things. To begin with, we see in this gradual restoration to sight, a vivid illustration of *the manner in which the Spirit frequently works in the conversion of souls*. We are all naturally blind and ignorant in matters which concern our souls. Conversion is an illumination, a change from darkness to light, from blindness to seeing the kingdom of God. Yet few converted people see things distinctly at first. It is not until the work of the Spirit has become deeper, and their experience more matured, that they see things with greater clarity. This is the history of thousands of God's children.

We then see further in this gradual cure of the blind man, a striking picture of *the present position of Christ's believing people in the world*, compared with that which is to come. We do not know the meaning of much that is happening around us and to us. In God's providential dealings with his children, and in the conduct of many of his saints, we see much that we cannot understand, and cannot alter. But we may look forward and take comfort. The time will come when things will become clear. 'The night is far gone; the day is at hand' (Romans 13:12). Let us be content to wait and watch, to work and pray. When the day of the Lord comes, our spiritual eyesight will be perfected. We shall see as we have been seen, and we shall know as we have been known.

8:27–33

The circumstances here recorded are of great importance. They took place during a journey Jesus and his disciples were making 'to the villages of Caesarea Philippi', and arose out of a conversation 'on the way'.

Observe firstly, *the variety of opinions about Christ* which prevailed among the Jews. Some held that he was John the Baptist, some Elijah, and some 'one of the prophets'. Every kind of opinion seemed to be current, except the one that was true.

We can see the same thing on every side at the present time. Christ and his gospel are just as little understood in reality, and are the subject of just as many different opinions, now, as they were then. Many know the name of Christ, but how many thoroughly realise that he is very God, the one mediator, the one high priest, the only source of life and peace, the shepherd and the friend? Vague ideas about him are still very common. May we never rest until we can say of Christ, 'My beloved is mine, and I am his' (Song of Songs 2:16).

Observe secondly, *the good confession of faith which the apostle Peter uttered*. To Jesus' question, 'Who do people say that I am?', Peter replied, 'You are the Christ.' This was a noble answer. Peter's faith was not stumbled by Jesus' poverty and low estate. His confidence was not shaken by the opposition of the scribes and Pharisees. None of these things moved him. He believed that he whom he followed, Jesus of Nazareth, was the promised Saviour, the true prophet greater than Moses, the long-predicted Messiah. And he declared it boldly and unhesitatingly.

Such bold confessions as Peter's are a true evidence of living faith, and are required in every age, if people will prove themselves to be Christ's disciples. We too must be ready to confess Christ as Peter did, and to do so with few on our side and many against us. Moreover, Jesus takes notice of those who confess him before men, and will one day confess them as his servants before an assembled world.

Observe thirdly, *the full declaration which our Lord makes of his own coming death and resurrection.* 'And he began to teach them that the Son of Man must suffer many things and be rejected by the elders and the chief priests and the scribes and be killed, and after three days rise again.'

The events announced here must have sounded strange to the disciples, and must have been heavy tidings to them and beyond their understanding. In what Jesus says, the word 'must' is striking. Why did he say 'must'? It cannot mean that he was unable to escape suffering, or that he had to die in order to give some great example to the world of self-sacrifice and self-denial. What he did mean is that his death and passion were necessary in order to make an atonement for men's sins, for 'without the shedding of blood there is no forgiveness of sins' (Hebrews 9:22). Without the sacrifice of his body on the cross, there could be no satisfaction to God's holy law, no reconciliation with God for the sinner, no taking away of sin, no gift of eternal life. In sum, Jesus must be 'delivered up for our trespasses and raised for our justification' (Romans 4:25).

Here is the central truth of the Bible. In comparison with this, all other truths are of secondary importance. Let us see that we have a firm grasp upon this truth, and ensure that it is always the foundation truth of our Christianity. In life and death, in health and sickness, let us lean all our weight on this mighty fact—that though we have sinned, Christ has died for sinners, and that though we deserve nothing, Christ has suffered on the cross for us, and by that suffering purchased heaven for all who believe in him.

Observe finally, *the strange mixture of grace and infirmity which may be found in the heart of a true Christian.* Peter, who had just made this strong confession of faith, presumed to rebuke his Master because he spoke of suffering and dying. As a result, Jesus responded to him with as sharp a rebuke as ever fell from his lips during his earthly ministry: 'Get behind me, Satan! For you are not setting your mind on the things of God, but on the things of man.'

What proof this gives us that the best of saints is a poor fallible creature. Here was *ignorance* in Peter: he did not understand the necessity of Jesus's death, and would actually have prevented his sacrifice on the cross. Here was *self-conceit* in Peter: he thought he knew what was right and fitting for his Master better than his Master himself, and actually undertook to show his Master a better way. And Peter did this with the *best intentions!* It is possible to mean well and yet fall into tremendous mistakes.

It is but a little step from making a good confession to being a 'Satan' in Christ's way. Let us learn humility from what happened here, and pray daily that the Lord will uphold, keep and teach us. And let us be charitable to our brethren who make errors and mistakes, remembering this Scripture counsel: 'Brothers, if anyone is caught in any transgression, you who are spiritual should restore him in a spirit of gentleness. Keep watch on yourself, lest you too be tempted' (Galatians 6:1).

8:34–38

The words of our Lord Jesus Christ in this passage are peculiarly weighty and solemn. They were spoken to correct the mistaken views of his disciples as to the nature of his kingdom; but they contain truths of the deepest importance to all Christians in all ages.

We learn, for one thing, *the absolute necessity of self-denial, if we would be Christ's disciples and be saved*. What does Jesus say? 'If anyone would come after me, let him deny himself and take up his cross and follow me.'

Salvation is without question all of grace, offered freely in the gospel to the chief of sinners, 'without money and without price' (Isaiah 55:1). 'For by grace you have been saved through faith. And this is not your own doing; it is the gift of God, not a result of works, so that no one may boast' (Ephesians 2:8–9). But all who accept this great salvation must prove the reality of their faith by carrying the cross after Christ. They must not think to enter heaven without trouble, pain, suffering and conflict on earth. They must be content to take up the cross of doctrine and the cross of practice—the cross of holding a faith which the world despises, and the cross of living a life which the world ridicules. They must be willing to mortify the deeds of the body, fight daily with the devil, come out from the world—and even to lose their lives, if needful—for Christ's sake and the gospel's. These are hard sayings, but they cannot be evaded. If we will not carry the cross, we shall never wear the crown.

However, do not let us ever be deterred from Christ's service by fear of this cross. Heavy as that cross may seem, Jesus will give us grace to bear it. We shall prove, with the apostle Paul, 'I can do all things through him who strengthens me' (Philippians 4:13). The cross is but for a few years, while the glory at the end is for evermore.

Let us ask ourselves regularly: does our Christianity cost us anything?—does it involve any sacrifice?—has it the true stamp of heaven?—does it carry with it any cross? If not, we may well tremble and be afraid, for a religion which costs nothing is worth nothing.

We learn, for another thing, *the unspeakable value of the soul*. What does Jesus say? 'For what does it profit a man to gain the whole world and forfeit his life?' These words are intended to stir us up to exertion and self-denial.

We all have souls that will live for evermore—souls which will live on when our bodies are in the grave—souls for which we shall have to give account to God. Yet what little attention so many give to anything except this world. Anyone may lose his own soul. He cannot save it—only Christ can do that. But he can lose it, and do so in many different ways: *murdering* it (by loving sin and cleaving to the world), *poisoning* it (by choosing a religion of lies and believing man-made superstitions), *starving* it (by neglecting all means of grace and refusing to receive the gospel into his heart). And the whole world cannot make up to anyone the loss of their soul.

Let these sayings of our Lord sink deep into our hearts, for words are inadequate to express their importance.

We learn, finally, *the great danger of being ashamed of Christ*. What does Jesus say? 'For whoever is ashamed of me and of my words in this adulterous and sinful generation, of him will the Son of Man also be ashamed when he comes in the glory of his Father with the holy angels.'

When can it be said of anyone, that he is ashamed of Christ? We are guilty of this when we are ashamed of letting people see that we believe and love the doctrines of Christ—that we desire to live according to the commandment of Christ—and that we wish to be counted among the people of Christ.

Perhaps there are few of Jesus' sayings which are more condemning than this. 'The fear of man lays a snare' (Proverbs 29:25). There are countless folk who would face all manner of dangers and demands and fear nothing, and yet would be ashamed of being thought 'religious', and would not dare to confess openly that they desired to please Christ rather than man.

Let us all pray daily for faith and courage to confess Christ before men. Of sin, worldliness or unbelief, we may well be ashamed. But we ought never to be ashamed of him who died for us on the cross. In spite of facing laughter, mockery and hard words, let us boldly assert that we serve Christ. Let us often look forward to the day of his second coming, and remember what he says in these verses. A thousand times better to confess Christ now and be despised by man, than be disowned by Christ before his Father on the day of judgment.

Chapter 9

9:1–13

The connection of this passage with the end of the previous one ought never to be overlooked. Jesus had been speaking of his own coming death and passion, of the necessity of self-denial if men would be his disciples, and of the need of losing our lives if we would have them saved. Now, in the same breath, he goes on to speak of his future kingdom and glory. He takes the edge off his 'hard sayings', by promising a sight of that glory to some of those who heard him.

Notice, firstly, *the marvellous vision of the glory which Christ and his people shall have at his second coming.* This was one of the chief purposes of the transfiguration. It was intended to teach the disciples that, though their Lord was lowly and poor in appearance now, he would one day appear in such royal majesty as became the Son of God—that, when their Master came the second time, his saints (like Moses and Elijah) would appear with him—and that, though reviled and persecuted now, because they belonged to Christ, they would one day be clothed with honour and be partakers of their Master's glory.

How thankful we should be for Jesus' transfiguration. We are often tempted to give up in Christ's service, because of the cross and affliction it involves. We see few with us, and many against us. All manner of evil is spoken against us, because we believe and love the gospel. So let us see in this episode a remedy for our doubting thoughts. Here is a gracious pledge that glorious things are in store for the people of God. Our crucified Saviour will come again in power and great glory—his saints will appear with him, and are safe in his keeping until that day. We may wait patiently. 'When Christ who is your life appears, then you also will appear with him in glory' (Colossians 3:34).

Notice, secondly, *the strong expression of the apostle Peter when he saw his Lord transfigured.* 'And Peter said to Jesus, "Rabbi, it is good that we are here."' What joy and happiness this glorious sight of Jesus, with Moses and Elijah, conferred on this warm-hearted disciple. And let us see in Peter's words, what comfort and consolation the sight of glory can give to a true believer. Let us look forward, and try to form some idea of the pleasure which Christians shall experience when they shall at last meet the Lord Jesus at his second coming, and meet to part no more. This experience of a short time was sufficient to warm and stir Peter's heart. Such was the sight, that he desired to enjoy more of it. What shall we say then, when we see our Lord appear at the last day with—not just two, but with all his saints? What shall we say, when we ourselves are allowed to share in Jesus' glory, and join the happy company, and feel that we shall go out no more from the joy of our Lord? The feelings of which Peter had a little foretaste will then be ours in full expression. We shall all say, with one heart and one voice, 'it is good that we are here'.

Notice, finally, *the distinct testimony which it bears to Christ's office and dignity as the promised Messiah*. We see this testimony in the appearance of Moses and Elijah, the representatives of the law and the prophets. They appear as witnesses that Jesus is the one of whom they spoke and wrote, that he would come. They disappear after a short while and leave Jesus alone—as though they would show that they are only witnesses, and that, Jesus having come, the servants resign to him the chief place.

We see this testimony also in the miraculous voice from heaven, saying 'This is my beloved Son; listen to him.' The same voice of God the Father, which was heard at Jesus' baptism, was heard once more at his transfiguration. On both occasions there was the same solemn declaration, 'This is my beloved Son.' On this occasion there was an addition of the important words, 'listen to him'.

The whole conclusion of this remarkable event was calculated to leave a lasting impression on the minds of the three disciples (Peter, James and John). It taught them, in the most striking manner, that their Lord was far above them and the prophets, just as the master of the house is above the servants—and that they must in all things believe, follow, obey and trust him. Him let us hear—in him let us abide—on him let us lean—to him let us look.

9:14–29

The contrast between these verses and the ones we have just been considering is very striking. We pass from the mount of transfiguration to a melancholy history of the work of the devil. We come down from the sight of glory to a conflict with Satanic possession. We exchange the blessed company of Moses and Elijah for the rough arguing of the unbelieving scribes. We leave the foretaste of the promised glory, and the solemn voice of God the Father testifying of God the Son, and return again to a scene of pain, weakness and misery—a boy in agony of body, a father in deep distress, and a little band of feeble disciples who were baffled by Satan's power and unable to give relief. Yet this is but a faint emblem of the change of scene that Jesus voluntarily undertook, when he first laid aside his glory and came into the world. And it is also a vivid picture of the life of all true Christians—scenes of weakness and sorrow being the rule, with only occasional foretastes of heaven and seasons on the mount.

Learn, first of all, *how dependent Christ's disciples are on the company and help of their Master.* When Jesus came down from the mountain he found his little flock in confusion. The nine apostles there were under pressure from a party of malicious scribes, and were failing in their attempt to heal one who had been brought to them possessed by a devil. They were learning by humbling experience the great lesson Jesus teaches, 'for apart from me you can do nothing' (John 15:5).

This has often been the experience of Christ's people in every age. The very ones who at one time have done great exploits in the cause of the gospel, at another time have failed entirely and proved weak and unstable as water. The holiest and best of Christians have nothing to boast of in themselves. So let us learn a lesson in humility from the disciples' failure here. Let us strive to realise every day our need of the grace and presence of Christ. With him we may do all things—without him we can do nothing at all.

Learn, in the second place, *how early in life we are liable to be injured by Satan.* The one upon whom Satan inflicted fearful miseries here was just a 'boy' who had been affected in this way since 'childhood'.

What an important lesson is here for us. We must labour to do good to our children even from their earliest years. If Satan begins so early to do them harm, we must not be behind him in seeking diligently to lead them to God. The devil, we may be sure, loses no time in endeavouring to influence the minds of children and young people, so we also should lose no time in speaking to them as moral beings and praying for their salvation. If young hearts can be filled by Satan, they can also be filled with the Spirit of God.

Learn, in the third place, *how faith and unbelief can be mixed together in the same heart.* The words of the child's father set this truth before us in a touching way. 'I believe; help my unbelief.'

We see here a vivid picture of the heart of many a true Christian. Few are found among believers in whom trust and doubt, hope and fear, do not exist side by side. Our knowledge, love and humility are all more or less defective and mingled with corruption. As it is with other graces, so it is with our faith. We believe, yet have about us a remainder of unbelief.

What, then, shall we do with our faith? We must *use it*, however weak, trembling, doubting or feeble it may be. We must not wait until it is perfect and mighty, but (like the man here) hope that one day it will become stronger: 'I believe.'

And what shall we do with our unbelief? We must *resist it*, and pray against it. We must take it to Christ, as we take all our other sins and infirmities, and cry to him for deliverance: 'help my unbelief'.

It is of the utmost importance to our comfort to know that a true believer may be known by his inward warfare as well as by his inward peace.

Learn, in the last place, *the complete dominion which our Lord exercises over Satan and all his agents.* The 'mute and deaf spirit' who was too strong for the disciples, is immediately cast out by the Master. Jesus speaks with mighty authority, and Satan at once is obliged to obey. 'I command you, come out of him and never enter him again.'

Greater is he who is for us than all those who are against us. Satan is strong, busy, active and full of malice. But Jesus 'is able to save to the uttermost those who draw near to God through him' (Hebrews 7:25). Jesus lives, and will never let Satan snatch us out of his hand. 'The God of peace will soon crush Satan under (our) feet' (Romans 16:20).

9:30–37

Mark here, firstly, *our Lord's renewed announcement of his own coming death and resurrection*. We read that 'he was teaching his disciples, saying to them, "The Son of Man is going to be delivered into the hands of men, and they will kill him. And when he is killed, after three days he will rise."'

The dullness of the disciples in spiritual things appears once more, as soon as this announcement was made. There was good in the tidings as well as seeming bad—sweet as well as bitter—life as well as death—the resurrection as well as the cross. 'But they did not understand the saying, and were afraid to ask him.' Their minds were still full of their mistaken ideas of their Master's reign upon earth.

The immense importance of Jesus' death and resurrection comes out strongly in what he says here. It is not for nothing that he reminds us again that he must die. He would have us know that his death was the great end for which he came into the world, and that by that death the great problem of how God could be just and yet justify sinners was to be solved. He did not come upon earth merely to teach, preach and work miracles, but to make satisfaction for sin by his own blood and suffering on the cross.

Mark here, secondly, *the ambition and love of pre-eminence which the apostles exhibited*. We read that 'on the way they had argued with one another about who was the greatest'. How strange this sounds! Who would have expected that poor men, who had given up all for Christ's sake, would have been troubled by strife and dissension, as to the place and precedence which each one deserved? Yet so it is.

It is an awful fact that pride is one of the most common sins which beset human nature. We all think better of ourselves than we ought, and all tend to imagine that we deserve something better than we have. It is an *old* sin, which began in the garden of Eden—a *subtle* sin, which dwells in many a heart without being detected—a *soul-ruining* sin, preventing repentance and keeping men back from Christ. Let us watch against it, and be on our guard.

Mark here, thirdly, *the peculiar standard of true greatness which our Lord sets before his disciples*. 'And he said to them, "If anyone would be first, he must be last of all and servant of all."'

These words show us that the priorities of the world are directly contrary to the mind of Christ. The world's idea of greatness is to rule, but Christian greatness consists in serving. The world's ambition is to receive honour and attention, but the desire of the Christian should be to give rather than to receive, and to attend on others rather than be attended on himself. Those who are willing to be the last of all and servants of all, for Christ's sake, are always few. Yet such a spirit constitutes true greatness in the eyes of Christ.

Mark here, finally, *what encouragement our Lord gives us to show kindness to the least and lowest who believe in his name*. He teaches this lesson very movingly. 'And he took a child and put him in the midst of them, and taking him in his arms, he said to them, "Whoever receives one such child in my name receives me, and whoever receives me, receives not me but him who sent me."'

The principle laid down here is a continuation of what we have just been considering, and is one which is foolishness to the natural man. Flesh and blood can see no other way to greatness than crowns, rank, wealth, and high position in the world. The Son of God declares that the way lies in devoting ourselves to the care of the weakest and lowest of the flock. Whatever the world may think, those who do this are the ones whom Jesus will delight to honour at the last day.

9:38–50

We see in these verses, *the mind of Christ on the great subject of toleration in religion*. 'John said to him, "Teacher, we saw someone casting out demons in your name, and we tried to stop him, because he was not following us."' Although the man was no doubt doing a good work and warring on the same side as the apostles, this did not satisfy John. Because the person in question was not working in the company of the apostles, John had forbidden him. But Jesus responds, 'Do not stop him, for no one who does a mighty work in my name will be able soon afterward to speak evil of me. For the one who is not against us is for us.'

Here is a golden rule, one too often forgotten. Men of all branches of Christ's church can be apt to think that only those of their own party or denomination can do any good in the world. They become narrow-minded and intolerant, and can see no merit in anyone else. Let us be on our guard against this attitude, which is often all too near the surface of all our hearts. We may think our fellow Christians mistaken in some points—but this must not prevent us from rejoicing if the works of the devil are destroyed and souls are saved. Far better that the work be done by other hands than not at all. Let us study to demonstrate the attitude which Jesus here commends.

We see, for another thing, *the need of giving up anything that stands between us and the salvation of our souls*. The 'hand' and 'foot' are to be cut off, and the 'eye' is to be torn out, if they offend or are occasions of falling and would injure our souls.

At first sight, this rule sounds stern and harsh, but our loving Master did not give it without cause. Compliance with it is absolutely necessary, since neglect of it is the sure way to hell. Bodily senses and members are good servants, when under right direction; but they need daily watching, lest they lead us into sin.

This is the advice of a wise physician, the counsel of a tender father, the warning of a faithful friend. However much folk may ridicule us for our strictness and preciseness, let us habitually be those who, belonging 'to Christ Jesus have crucified the flesh with its passions and desires' (Galatians 5:24). Let us walk in the steps of Job ('I have made a covenant with my eyes', Job 31:1) and of Paul ('But I discipline my body and keep it under control, lest after preaching to others I myself should be disqualified', 1 Corinthians 9:27).

We see, in the last place, *the reality, awfulness, and eternity of future punishment*. Three times the Lord Jesus speaks of 'hell', as well as speaking of 'where their worm does not die and the fire is not quenched'.

These are awful expressions and need to be pondered and remembered. There is a real hell, and that hell is eternal. There is no kindness in keeping back from people the subject of hell. Fearful and tremendous as it is, it ought to be pressed on all, as one of the great truths of Christianity. Our loving Saviour speaks frequently of it. Were there no boundless mercy in Christ for all who believe in him, we might well shrink from such a topic—were there no precious blood of Christ able to cleanse away all sin, we might well keep silent about the wrath to come. But there is mercy for all who ask in Christ's name—there is a fountain open for all sin. So let us then, boldly and unhesitatingly, maintain that there is a hell, and plead with sinners to flee from it, before it is too late. 'Therefore, knowing the fear of the Lord, we persuade others' (2 Corinthians 5:11). It is never possible to say too much about Christ; but it is quite possible to say too little about hell.

Before leaving this passage, let Jesus' concluding words ring in our ears: 'Have salt in yourselves, and be at peace with one another.' Let us ensure that we have in our hearts the saving grace of the Holy Spirit—sanctifying, purifying, preserving from corruption, our whole inward being. Let us watch the grace given to us with daily watchfulness, praying to be kept from carelessness and sin—lest we be overtaken in faults, bring misery on our consciences, and discredit our profession. Above all, let us live in 'peace with one another'—never seeking great things for ourselves or striving for the pre-eminence, but clothed with humility, and loving all who love Christ in sincerity.

Chapter 10

10:1–12

The opening verse of this passage shows us *the patient perseverance of our Lord Jesus Christ as a teacher*. 'And he left there and went to the region of Judea and beyond the Jordan, and the crowds gathered to him again. And again, as his custom was, he taught them.'

Wherever Jesus went, he was always about his Father's business—preaching, teaching, and labouring to do good to souls. He never threw away an opportunity. In the entire history of his earthly ministry, we never read of an idle day. And yet he knew the hearts of all men, and that the great proportion of his hearers were hardened and unbelieving—that most of his words fell to the ground uncared for and unheeded—and that so far as concerned the salvation of souls, much of his labour appeared to be in vain. Yet still, knowing all this, he laboured on.

Here is provided a standing pattern for us all. Let every Christian (minister, missionary, Sunday school teacher, evangelist, head of a home, and every other believer) remember Christ's example and resolve to do likewise. We are not to give up, just because we see no good done—we are not to relax our efforts, because we see no visible fruit—we are to work on steadily, keeping before us the great principle that while the duty is ours, the results are God's. It is to the 'good and faithful servant' to whom the Lord Jesus will say, at the last day, 'Enter into the joy of your master' (Matthew 25:21).

The greater portion of this passage is given to show us *the dignity and importance of the relation of marriage*. It is clear that the prevailing opinions of the Jews upon this subject, when Jesus was here upon earth, were lax and low in the extreme. The binding character of the marriage bond was not recognised. Divorce for slight and trivial causes was both allowed and common among them. The mutual duties of husbands and wives regarding one another were little understood. So, in order to correct this state of things, our Lord sets up a high and holy standard of principles, making it clear as he does so that Moses' allowing of 'a man to write a certificate of divorce and to send (his wife) away', was itself a proof of the people's 'hardness of heart' and that they had fallen so far below God's original standard of marriage.

Jesus quotes and endorses the solemn words used at the marriage of Adam and Eve, as words of perpetual significance: 'Therefore a man shall leave his father and mother and hold fast to his wife, and they shall become one flesh.' He then adds a solemn comment to these words: 'What therefore God has joined together, let not man separate.' Finally, in reply to the inquiry of the disciples ('And in the house the disciples asked him again about this matter'), he declared to them that divorce followed by remarriage, except for the cause of marital unfaithfulness, is a breach of the seventh commandment (compare the parallel passage in Matthew 19:9, and also Matthew 5:32).

The importance of Jesus' teaching on this subject can hardly be overstated, and it would be well for all who are married, or are considering marriage, to ponder it carefully. Of all relations of life, none ought to be regarded with such reverence, and none embarked upon so carefully, as the relation of husband and wife. There is the greatest happiness to be found if it be entered upon in the true fear of God—yet much misery to be faced if it is taken in hand without thought. Moreover, the nearer a nation's laws about marriage approach to the law of Christ, the higher has the moral tone of that nation always proved to be.

Happy are those who, in the matter of marriage, observe three rules. The *first* is for Christians to marry only in the Lord, and after prayer for God's approval and blessing. The *second* is to remember that marriage is the union of two sinners, and not of two angels. The *third* is to strive first and foremost for one another's sanctification, for the more holy married people are, the happier they are.

10:13–16

The scene brought before us here is deeply interesting. We read of children being brought to Jesus 'that he might touch them', and of the disciples rebuking those who brought them. However, 'when Jesus saw it, he was indignant', and he rebuked his disciples in a marked manner. Then, with regard to the children, 'he took them in his arms and blessed them, laying his hands on them'.

An important matter we learn from these verses is *how much attention the souls of children should receive from the church of Christ*. The great 'head over all things to the church' (Ephesians 1:22) found time to take special notice of children. Although his time on earth was precious, and grown-up men and women were perishing around him on every side, he did not consider boys and girls of small importance, and had room in his mighty heart for them. And he has left on record his words concerning them, that 'to such belongs the kingdom of God'.

We must never allow ourselves to suppose that children's (even little children's) souls may be safely left alone. They are never too young to learn evil and sin—never too young to receive spiritual impressions—never too young to think about God, their souls, and a world to come. They each have a conscience, and a soul which will live for ever in heaven or hell. We cannot endeavour too soon to bring them to Christ.

It is the bounden duty of every Christian congregation to make provision for the spiritual training of children, and we may confidently expect the Lord's blessing on all attempts to do them good.

[To be fair to Ryle, it must be noted that he then proceeds to draw a second matter from these verses, namely, *how much encouragement there is to bring young children to be baptised*. This is, of course, a matter to which many Christians adhere, and many do not, all of them prayerful students of the Scriptures. Ryle does acknowledge that 'it is not pretended that there is any mention of baptism' here, but urges that 'the expressions and gestures of our Lord in this passage, are a strong indirect argument in favour of infant baptism', and then proceeds (in a gracious manner) to develop that thought. His final paragraph on this section is both important and helpful. It now follows.

The baptism that it concerns us all to know, is not so much the baptism of water as the baptism of the Holy Spirit. Thousands are washed in baptismal waters who are never renewed by the Spirit. Have we been born again? Have we received the Holy Spirit, and been made new creatures in Jesus Christ? If not, it matters little when, and where, and how we have been baptised; we are still in our sins. Without a new birth there can be no salvation. May we never rest until we know and feel that we have passed from death to life, and are indeed born of God!]

10:17–27

The instance recorded here (found in Matthew, Mark and Luke) teaches lessons deserving particular notice.

Learn, for one thing, *the self-ignorance of man*. We are told of a man who 'ran up' to Jesus, 'and knelt before him', and then asked him the solemn question, 'what must I do to inherit eternal life?' At first sight, his case appears promising. He showed anxiety about spiritual things, while so many around him were careless and indifferent, and adopted a reverent manner before the Lord, unlike the scribes and Pharisees. Yet, at the same time, the man was profoundly ignorant of his own heart. He heard Jesus recite those commandments which set out our duty to our neighbour, and immediately asserted, 'all these I have kept from my youth'. He appears utterly unacquainted with the searching nature of God's moral law, and its application to our thoughts and words, as well as our actions.

The spiritual blindness exhibited here is, unhappily, very common. Myriads, even of professing Christians, have no idea of their own sinfulness and guilt in the sight of God. They flatter themselves on not having done anything wicked, like murdering or committing adultery. Yet they forget the holy nature of that God with whom they have to do. They forget (for example) how often they break God's law in temper or imagination, even when their outward conduct is correct. As a result, they are wrapped up in self-righteousness, and in that state they live, and sometimes die.

Let us beware of this state of mind, and pray for self-knowledge. Let us ask the Holy Spirit to convince us of our sin, show us our own hearts, show us God's holiness, and show us our need of Christ. Whoever's eyes have really been opened to the spirituality of the commandments, will never rest until they have found Christ.

Learn, for another thing, *the love of Christ towards sinners.* This is brought out in the words, 'And Jesus, looking at him, loved him.' That love, beyond doubt, was a love of compassion, as Jesus beheld the strange mixture of earnestness and ignorance which the man demonstrated.

We must never forget that Jesus feels love and compassion for the souls of the ungodly. Certainly, he feels a peculiar love for those who hear his voice and follow him, for they are his sheep, given to him by the Father, and watched with a special care—and they are his bride, joined to him in an everlasting covenant, and dear to him as part of himself. But the heart of Jesus is a wide heart, with an abundance of tender concern even for those who are following sin and the world. He who wept over unbelieving Jerusalem is still the same. This being so, we may boldly tell the chief of sinners that Christ loves him. Salvation is ready for the worst of men, if they will only come to Christ.

Learn, in the last place, *the immense danger of the love of money.* With all his professed desire after eternal life, this man loved his money more than his soul. We are told, 'he went away sorrowful, for he had great possessions'. Following this, 'Jesus looked around and said to his disciples, "How difficult it will be for those who have wealth to enter the kingdom of God."' These words amazed the disciples, and warn us all to watch against the love of money, and to pray for contentment with such things as we have, whether we are rich or poor. The highest wisdom is to be of one mind with the apostle Paul: 'I have learned in whatever situation I am to be content' (Philippians 4:11).

10:28–34

Notice first of all, here, *the glorious promise which these verses contain.* Jesus says to his apostles, 'Truly, I say to you, there is no one who has left house or brothers or sisters or mother or father or children or lands, for my sake and for the gospel, who will not receive a hundredfold now in this time, houses and brothers and sisters and mothers and children and lands, with persecutions, and in the age to come eternal life.'

There are few wider promises than this in the word of God, particularly in terms of holding out encouragement for the present life. Here is a promise for any and all who are fearful or faint-hearted in Christ's service, or who are enduring hardness and tribulation for his sake. The promise is not only of pardon and glory in the world to come, but of blessings even here and now which more than compensate for all that is lost: 'a hundredfold now in this time'. Such blessings include new friends, relatives and companions in the family of Christ, and countless numbers have discovered by experience that this promise is true. And as soon as those who make sacrifices on account of the gospel come to die, there is 'in the age to come eternal life'. The afflictions of the present will end in an everlasting reward. All their fights and sorrows endured here will be exchanged for perfect rest and a conqueror's crown. All the former things will have passed away, and God will make 'all things new' (Revelation 21:5).

Let us wait patiently on the Lord, for while 'Weeping may tarry for the night', yet 'joy comes with the morning' (Psalm 30:5).

Notice, here, in the second place, *the solemn warning which these verses contain.* Jesus saw the secret self-conceit of his apostles, and gave them a word in season to check their high thoughts. 'But many who are first will be last, and the last first.'

How true these words were, when applied to the twelve apostles. There stood among them one who would fall away and come to a disgraceful end—Judas Iscariot. Equally, there did not stand among them then one who, at a later time, did more for Christ than any of the twelve—Saul of Tarsus.

How true these words are, when we apply them to the history of Christian churches. There are places in the world where once the church of Christ flourished, yet does so no longer. And there are places where at one time the church of Christ did not exist, yet now prospers.

How true these words are, when applied to believers. There are those who once appeared to run well, but where are they now? The world has got hold of one, false doctrine has captured another, moral fall has ruined another. Yet others, who once did not profess Christ at all, are now vigorous in their service and testimony for the Lord.

We all need to pray for humility in the light of these words of Jesus. It is not enough to begin well. We must persevere, press on, and not grow weary, concerned to bear the good fruit of settled habits of repentance, faith and holiness. Happy is the person who counts the cost, and resolves, having once begun to walk in the narrow way, by God's grace never to turn aside.

Notice here, finally, *our Lord's clear foreknowledge of his own suffering and death*. Calmly and deliberately, Jesus tells his disciples of his coming passion in Jerusalem. One after another he describes all the leading circumstances which would attend his death. Nothing is kept back.

Mark this well: there was nothing unforeseen in Jesus' death. From the beginning of his earthly ministry he saw the cross before him, and went to it as a willing sufferer. He knew that his death was the necessary payment that must be made in order to reconcile God and man. That payment he had covenanted and engaged to make at the price of his own blood—so when the appointed time came, he kept his word, and died for our sins on Calvary.

Let us ceaselessly praise God that the gospel sets before us such a Saviour—so faithful to the terms of the covenant, so willing to bear a curse in our place. And let us never doubt that he who fulfilled his engagement to suffer, will also fulfil his engagement to save all who come to him. Let us not only accept him as our Redeemer and Advocate, but gladly give ourselves, and all that we have, to his service. Surely, if Jesus died for us, it is a small thing to require Christians to live for him.

10:35–45

Notice, firstly, *the ignorance of our Lord's disciples*. We find James and John requesting first places in the kingdom of glory: 'Grant us to sit, one at your right hand and one at your left, in your glory.' And we find them confidently declaring their ability to drink of their Master's cup and be baptised with their Master's baptism. With all their faith and grace, and their love to Jesus, they knew neither their own hearts nor the nature of the path before them.

There are few true Christians who do not resemble James and John, when they first begin the service of Christ. We are apt to forget the cross and the tribulation, and think only of the crown. We form an incorrect estimate of our own patience and power of endurance. We misjudge our own ability to withstand temptation and trial. As a result, we offer learn by bitter experience, after many disappointments and not a few falls.

Let the case before us teach us the importance of a solid and calm judgment in our Christian life. Like James and John, we are right in telling all our desires to Jesus, and right in believing that he is King of kings. But let us not, as they did, forget that there is a cost to be borne by every Christian, and that 'through many tribulations we must enter the kingdom of God' (Acts 14:22).

Notice, secondly, *what praise our Lord bestows on lowliness, and devotion to the good of others.* We learn that 'when the ten heard it, they began to be indignant at James and John', not liking the thought of anyone being placed above themselves. Jesus was aware of their feelings, and, like a wise physician, proceeded at once to apply a corrective medicine. He told them that their ideas of greatness were built on a mistaken foundation, and repeated with renewed emphasis the lesson laid down in the previous chapter—that 'whoever would be great among you must be your servant'. And he backs this up with the overwhelming argument of his own example: 'For even the Son of Man came not to be served but to serve.'

Let all who desire to please Christ, watch and pray against self-esteem. It is a feeling deeply rooted in our hearts. Many a time Christians have felt irritated and annoyed when a brother has been more honoured than themselves. We ought often to ponder these words: 'Do nothing from rivalry or conceit, but in humility count others more significant than yourselves' (Philippians 2:3). Blessed is that servant of Christ who can sincerely rejoice when others are exalted, though he himself is overlooked and passed by. Let all who desire to walk in Christ's steps labour to be useful to others, laying themselves out to do good in their day and generation.

Notice, lastly, *the language which our Lord uses in speaking of his own death.* He says of himself, that he came 'to give his life as a ransom for many'. This is an expression which ought to be carefully treasured up in the minds of all true Christians. It proves, without question, the atoning character of Jesus' death—a death which was no common death, but the payment of the debts of sinful man to a holy God—the ransom which Jesus undertook to provide, in order to procure liberty for sinners, tied and bound by the chain of their sins—the death by which Jesus made a full and complete satisfaction for man's countless transgressions—that death by which Christ 'himself bore our sins in his body on the tree' (1 Peter 2:24).

Let all those who trust in Christ take comfort in the thought that they build on a sure foundation, and may all such know this privilege of Christ's ransom by heartfelt experience, and walk in the blessed liberty of the children of God.

10:46–52

These verses narrate one of Jesus' miracles, in which we find a vivid emblem of spiritual things.

In the first place, we have here *an example of strong faith*. We are told that as Jesus 'was leaving Jericho with his disciples', a blind man named Bartimaeus 'was sitting by the roadside'. When this man 'heard that it was Jesus of Nazareth, he began to cry out and say, "Jesus, Son of David, have mercy on me!"'

Bartimaeus was blind in body, but not in soul. The eyes of his understanding were open. He saw that Jesus of Nazareth was the Son of David, the Messiah of whom prophets had prophesied long ago. He had not been able to witness any of Jesus' mighty miracles, but he had heard the report of these things, and hearing had believed.

Let us pray to have like precious faith. We too were not allowed to see Jesus with our bodily eyes, but we have the report of his power, his grace, and his willingness to save, in the gospel. We have great promises from his own lips, written down for our encouragement. Let us trust these promises absolutely, and commit our souls to Jesus unhesitatingly. What is the beginning of all saving faith, but a soul's venture on Christ? What is the life of saving faith, when once begun, but a continual leaning on an unseen Saviour's word? 'Though you have not seen him, you love him. Though you do not now see him, you believe in him and rejoice with joy that is inexpressible and filled with glory' (1 Peter 1:8).

We have, in the second place, *an example of determined perseverance in the face of difficulties.* When Bartimaeus began to cry out to Jesus, 'many rebuked him, telling him to be silent'. He received no encouragement from those near him. But that did not stop him. Rather, when this happened, 'he cried out all the more'—and so crying, he obtained his heart's desire, and received his sight.

Let all who wish to be saved, mark well this conduct of Bartimaeus, and walk diligently in his steps. Like him, we must care nothing what others think and say of us, when we seek the healing of our souls. There will always be people telling us it is too soon, too late, too this and too that, and that we need not be so anxious about salvation. We must pay no attention to them, but, rather, cry all the more that the Lord Jesus would have mercy on us.

Why are so many people so easily put off in seeking Christ, in drawing near to God? The answer is short and simple. They do not feel sufficiently their own sins—they are not thoroughly convinced of the plague of their own hearts, and the disease of their own souls. Once let someone see his own guilt as it really is, and he will never rest until he has found pardon and peace in Christ.

In the last place, we have *an example of the compelling influence which gratitude to Christ ought to have upon our souls.* Bartimaeus did not return home as soon as his sight was restored. He would not leave the one from whom he had received such mercy. At once, he devoted the new powers which his cure gave him, to the Son of David who had worked the cure. He 'followed him on the way'.

Let us see in these words a lively emblem of the effect that the grace of Christ should have on everyone who tastes it. It ought to make them followers of Jesus all their lives, and draw them with mighty power into the way of holiness. Freely pardoned, they should give themselves freely and willingly to Christ's service. Bought at so mighty a price as the blood of Christ, all should devote themselves heartily and thoroughly to him who redeemed them. Grace truly experienced will make a Christian feel daily, 'What shall I render to the LORD for all his benefits to me?' (Psalm 116:12).

Chapter 10

Have we had our eyes opened by the Spirit of God? Have we yet been taught to see sin, and Christ, and holiness, and heaven, in their true light? Can we say, 'One thing I do know, that though I was blind, now I see' (John 9:25)?

Chapter 11

11:1–11

The event described in these verses is an exception in the course of our Lord's earthly ministry. Generally speaking, we see him withdrawing himself from public notice. Here, however, he appears to drop his private character, and of his own choice to call public attention to himself, making a very visible entry into Jerusalem, with his disciples. Voluntarily, he rides into the city, surrounded by a great multitude of 'those who went before and those who followed after', who 'were shouting "Hosanna"', like king David returning to his palace in triumph (2 Samuel 19:40). And this was done at a time when countless Jews were gathered in Jerusalem, to keep the Passover.

Observe, firstly, *how public our Lord purposely made the last act of his life*. He came to Jerusalem to die, and he desired that all Jerusalem should know it. He drew the attention of rulers, priests, elders, scribes and Romans to himself, knowing that the most wonderful event that ever happened in this world was about to take place. The eternal Son of God was about to suffer in the place of sinful men—the great sacrifice for sin was about to be offered up—the great Passover Lamb was about to be slain—the great atonement for a world's sin was about to be made. He therefore ordered it so that his death was a public death, that the eyes of all Jerusalem were fixed upon him, and that, when he died, it was before many witnesses.

Let us be sure to see here one more proof of the unspeakable importance of the death of Christ. From that death flow all our hopes. Without that death we should have nothing solid beneath our feet. May we prize that death more and more every year that we live, and, in all our thoughts of Christ, rejoice in nothing so much as the great fact that he died for us.

Observe, secondly, *the voluntary poverty which our Lord underwent when he was upon earth*. How did he enter Jerusalem on this remarkable occasion? Did he come in a royal chariot, with horses, soldiers, and a retinue all around him, like kings of this world? Not at all. We learn that he borrowed a colt, and, for a saddle, sat on the disciples' cloaks. This was in perfect keeping with the character of his ministry.

We have here, an instance of that marvellous union of weakness and power (see 2 Corinthians 13:4), of riches and poverty, of the Godhead and the manhood, which may so often be traced in the history of the Lord Jesus. Who that reads the Gospels carefully can fail to observe, that he who could feed thousands with a few loaves, was himself sometimes hungry—he who could heal the sick and infirm, was himself sometimes weary—he who could cast out devils with a word, was himself tempted—and he who could raise the dead, could himself submit to die? So here—the power of our Lord in his triumphal entry into Jerusalem, along with the poverty of our Lord in his borrowing an ass to carry him when he made that triumphal entry.

This is all so very fitting. If we saw only his divine acts, we might forget that he was a man. If we saw only his seasons of poverty and weakness, we might forget that he was God. But we are intended to see in Jesus divine strength and human weakness united in one person. He is able to sympathise with us, because he is man; he is almighty to save us, because he is God.

11:12–21

We see in the beginning of this passage, *one of the many proofs that our Lord Jesus Christ was really man*. We are told that 'he was hungry'. He had a nature and bodily constitution like our own in all things, sin only excepted. He could weep, rejoice and suffer pain. He could be weary and need rest, thirsty and need drink, hungry and need food.

These truths should teach us the condescension of Christ. He who is the eternal God, and who made the world and all that it contains—he, even he, was pleased to suffer hunger, when he came into the world to save sinners. This is a great mystery. And these truths should teach us also Christ's power to sympathise with his believing people on earth, for he knows our sorrows by experience and can be touched with the feeling of our infirmities. When we tell him of our concerns in prayer, he knows what we mean and is no stranger to our troubles. Surely this is the very Saviour and Friend that poor aching, groaning, human nature requires.

We see here, secondly, *the great danger of unfruitfulness and formality in religion.* Jesus teaches this lesson in a remarkable fashion. 'And seeing in the distance a fig tree in leaf, he went to see if he could find anything on it. When he came to it, he found nothing but leaves.' He then pronounced upon it the solemn sentence, 'May no one ever eat fruit from you again.' The next day the fig tree was found 'withered away to its roots'.

This action of Jesus was a sermon of threefold application. Though withered and dried up, that fig tree still speaks. First, it speaks to the Jewish church. Rich in the leaves of a formal religion, but barren of all spiritual fruit, that church was in fearful danger, at the very time when this withering took place. Next, it speaks to all branches of Christ's visible church in every age and in every part of the world—warning against an empty profession of Christianity unaccompanied by sound doctrine and holy living. Above all, it speaks to all carnal, hypocritical, and false-hearted Christians—those who 'have the reputation of being alive,' yet 'are dead' (Revelation 3:1).

We must each take care to learn from the fig tree, that we must bear fruit to the glory of God. There must be fruit in our hearts and fruit in our lives, the fruit 'of repentance toward God and of faith in our Lord Jesus Christ' (Acts 20:21), with true holiness in every part of our conduct.

We see here, lastly, *how reverently we ought to use places which are set apart for public worship.* We learn this lesson from the striking manner of our Lord's conduct when he went into the temple: 'he began to drive out those who sold and those who bought in the temple, and he overturned the tables of the money-changers and the seats of those who sold pigeons'. And we are told that he enforced this action by warrant of Scripture: 'Is it not written, "My house shall be called a house of prayer for all the nations?" But you have made it a den of robbers.'

There is surely a particular reverence which is due to a place where Christ and his people meet together regularly and public prayer is offered up. Jesus takes notice of men's behaviour in places of worship, and all irreverence or profanity is an offence in his sight. So when we go to the house of God, let us go in a serious frame—calling to mind where we are, what we are doing, and in whose presence we are found.

11:22–26

Let us learn from these words of our Lord Jesus Christ, *the immense importance of faith*. This is a lesson which he teaches first by a proverbial saying. Faith shall enable a person to accomplish works and overcome difficulties as great and formidable as removing mountains, and throwing them into the sea. This lesson is then impressed upon us further, by Jesus' general exhortation to exercise faith when we pray: 'Therefore I tell you, whatever you ask in prayer, believe that you have received it, and it will be yours.' This promise must, of course, be taken with a reasonable qualification—that a believer will ask things which are not sinful, and which are in accordance with the will of God.

The faith commended here must be distinguished from that faith which is essential to justification. Although all true faith is always trust and belief, yet this distinction is important. Justifying faith is that act of the soul by which a sinner lays hold on Christ, and has peace with God. The faith spoken of in the present passage, however, is a grace which, while the fruit and companion of justifying faith, is not to be confused with it. It is a confidence in God's power, wisdom and goodwill to all believers. And its special objects are the promises, word and character of God in Christ.

Do we desire to 'grow in the grace and knowledge of our Lord and Saviour Jesus Christ' (2 Peter 3:18)? Do we wish to make progress in our Christian life, and become strong Christians, not remaining mere babes? Then let us pray daily for more faith, and watch our faith with most jealous watchfulness. According to our faith will be the degree of our peace, our hope, our joy, our decision in Christ's service, our boldness in confession, our strength in work, our patience in trial, our resignation in trouble, our felt comfort in prayer.

Let us learn, for another thing, from these verses, *the absolute necessity of a forgiving spirit towards others*. The connecting link here between the importance of faith (of which Jesus has just been speaking) and the forgiving of injuries, is prayer. Having been taught that faith is essential to the success of our prayers, it is now added that no prayers can be heard which do not come from a forgiving heart. 'And whenever you stand praying, forgive, if you have anything against anyone, so that your Father who also is in heaven may forgive you your trespasses.'

The value of our prayers, we can all understand, depends very much on the state of mind in which we offer them. Yet as well as being earnest, fervent, sincere, and in the name of Christ, our prayers must contain another ingredient: they must come from a forgiving heart. We have no right to look for mercy from God, if we are not ready to extend mercy to our brethren. We cannot really feel the sinfulness of the sins we ask God to pardon, if we cherish malice towards our fellows. We must not flatter ourselves that we 'have received the Spirit of adoption' (Romans 8:15), if we cannot bear and forbear.

We need to leave the passage with serious self-inquiry. Do we know what it is to be of a forgiving spirit? Can we overlook the injuries we receive from time to time in this evil world? Can we pass over a transgression and pardon an offence? If not, where is our Christianity? Let us determine, by God's grace, to forgive, even as we hope to be forgiven.

11:27–33

Observe firstly, here, *how much spiritual blindness may be in the hearts of those who hold office in churches.* We find 'the chief priests and the scribes and the elders' coming to Jesus, and raising difficulties and objections in the way of his work. These men were the accredited teachers and rulers of the Jewish church, and were regarded by the Jews as the fountain of religious knowledge. Yet we find them—the very ones who ought to have been instructors to others—full of prejudice against the truth, and bitter enemies of the Messiah.

These things are recorded to show Christians that they must beware of depending too much on men. Their acts and teaching must always be tested by the word of God, and they must be followed only so far as they follow Scripture, and no further. In the Lord Jesus alone is no weakness, no failure and no shadow of infirmity.

Observe, secondly, *how envy and unbelief make men throw discredit on the commission of those who work for God.* These chief priests and the others with them could not deny the reality of Jesus' miracles of mercy. They could not say that his teaching was contrary to Scripture, or that his life was sinful. So what did they do? They attacked his authority: 'By what authority are you doing these things, or who gave you this authority to do them?'

Without doubt, as a general principle, all who undertake to teach others should be properly appointed to the work. Yet it is one thing to maintain the lawfulness of an outward call to minister in sacred things, and quite another to assert that it is the only thing needful. There must be an inward call of the Holy Spirit, along with the outward call from men. It is important to ask: 'Is a man for Christ or against him? What does he teach? How does he live? Is he doing good?' We must remember that a physician is useless—however high his qualifications—if he cannot cure diseases; and a soldier is useless—however well dressed and drilled—if he will not face the enemy on the day of battle. The best doctor is the one who can cure, and the best soldier is the one who can fight.

Observe, finally, *what dishonesty and evasiveness unbelievers may be led into by prejudice against the truth.* Jesus responded to his questioners by asking them a question in return: 'Was the baptism of John from heaven or from man?' They dared not answer him—for if they said, 'from man', they were afraid of what the people would think of them, while if they said, 'from heaven', they knew Jesus would ask them why they did not then believe him. So they told a direct lie, and 'answered Jesus, "We do not know."'

It is a sad fact, that dishonesty like this is far from uncommon among unconverted people. So many will evade appeals to their conscience by answers which are not true. When pressed to attend to their souls, they say things which they know are not correct. They love the world and their own way, and like our Lord's enemies are determined not to give them up, but, like them, are ashamed also to tell the truth. One person pretends that he cannot understand the doctrines of the gospel—another insists that he tries to serve God, but makes no progress—yet another declares that he has every desire to serve Christ, but has no time. So much of the time, answers like these are as worthless as the answer given here to Jesus: 'We do not know.'

The plain truth is that we ought to be very slow to give credit to the unconverted person's professed reasons for not serving Christ. Much of the time, his 'I cannot' really means 'I will not.' The ruin of countless numbers of people is simply this: that they will not deal honestly with their own souls. They allege pretended difficulties in the way of their not serving Christ, while in reality they love 'the darkness rather than the light' (John 3:19), and have no honest desire to change.

Chapter 12

12:1–12

These verses contain an historical parable, in which the history of the Jewish nation—from the time Israel left Egypt until the destruction of Jerusalem—is set before us. Jesus uses the figure of the vineyard and the tenants to tell this story. Let us study it attentively, and apply it to ourselves.

Observe, firstly, *God's special kindness to the Jewish church and nation*. He gave to them peculiar privileges—including good laws and ordinances, a good land, casting out nations before them, passing by greater and mightier nations to show them favour—and dealt with them as someone who deals with a piece of land which he separates and hedges in for 'a vineyard'. No family under heaven ever received so many distinguishing privileges as the family of Abraham.

And we too, in Great Britain, have received many special mercies from God. Let us be thankful for our mercies, and know the hand from which they have come. Let us humble ourselves before God, lest we so provoke him as to take all these mercies away.

Observe, secondly, *God's patience and longsuffering towards the Jewish nation*. What is their whole history as recorded in the Old Testament, but a long record of repeated provocations and repeated pardons? Over and over again we read of prophets being sent to them and warnings being delivered, but all too often entirely in vain. One servant after another came to the vineyard and asked for fruit, yet no fruit was borne by the nation to the glory of God: 'they kept mocking the messengers of God, despising his words and scoffing at his prophets, until the wrath of the LORD rose against his people, until there was no remedy' (2 Chronicles 36:16). Never was there a people so patiently dealt with as Israel.

And we too, in Great Britain, have much longsuffering of God to be thankful for—abundant cause to say that our Lord is patient. We have often provoked him, yet his longsuffering and lovingkindness continue still. Let us beware lest we presume on his goodness too far. Let us hear in his mercies a loud call to us to bear fruit—let us strive to abound in that righteousness which 'exalts a nation' (Proverbs 14:34)—that the whole nation may yet be seen showing forth his praise.

Observe, thirdly, *the hardness and wickedness of human nature, as exemplified in the history of the Jewish people.* The summary of Israel's dealings with God's messengers, which Jesus sketches in this parable, affords striking proof of this. Prophet after prophet was sent to them in vain. The Son of God, himself, the 'beloved son', at last came down to them, and was not believed. God himself was manifest in the flesh, dwelling among them, and 'they took him and killed him'.

There is no truth so little realised and believed as the desperate wickedness of the human heart. This parable shows what men and women can do—in the full blaze of religious privileges, in the midst of prophecies and miracles, in the presence of the Son of God himself. 'For the mind that is set on the flesh in hostile to God' (Romans 8:7). Though Jesus became a man and lived upon earth, yet men would not have him, they rebelled against him, and at last they killed him. Let us put away the common notion that seeing and knowing what is good is enough to make a person a Christian. Nothing but the Spirit of God can change the heart. We 'must be born again' (John 3:7).

Observe, finally, *that men's consciences may be pricked, and yet they may continue impenitent.* The Jews, to whom Jesus addressed this solemn parable, saw clearly that it applied to themselves. They felt that they and their forefathers were 'the tenants' to whom 'the vineyard' was let, and who ought to have rendered fruit to God—that they and their forefathers were the wicked labourers who had refused to give the owner of the vineyard his dues, and had shamefully treated his servants, beating some and killing others—and that they themselves were planning the last crowning act of wickedness, in killing the 'beloved son' and throwing him 'out of the vineyard'. It is recorded that 'they perceived that he had told the parable against them'. Yet, though convicted by their own consciences, they were hardened in sin and would not repent.

Let us learn from this that knowledge and conviction alone cannot save any man's soul. It is quite possible to know that we are wrong, and be unable to deny it, yet to cling obstinately to our sins and perish miserably in hell. What we all need is a change of heart and will. For this, let us pray earnestly. Without this, we shall never be real Christians and reach heaven.

12:13–17

Let us observe here, first of all, *how men of different religious opinions can unite in opposing Christ*. We read of 'some of the Pharisees and some of the Herodians' coming together 'to trap (Jesus) in his talk'. The Pharisees were superstitious formalists, who only cared for the outward ceremonies of religion. The Herodians were mere men of the world, who despised all religion, and cared more for pleasing men than pleasing God. Yet when Jesus came among them, attacking the ruling passions of both alike, and sparing neither the formalist or the worldling, we find them making common cause against him.

It has always been so from the beginning of the world, and continues to the present day. Although worldly people and formalists have little real sympathy with one another, they share a dislike for the pure gospel of Jesus Christ. So whenever there is an opportunity to oppose the gospel, they are ready to combine and act together. We must never rely on their divisions, for they will always patch up an alliance to resist Christ.

Let us observe, for another thing, *the exceeding subtlety of the question put to our Lord*. His enemies asked him, 'Is it lawful to pay taxes to Caesar, or not? Should we pay them, or should we not?' Here was a question which seems at first sight an impossible one to answer without peril. If Jesus had told them to pay these taxes to the emperor, the Pharisees would have accused him before the priests as one who regarded the Jewish nation as being subject to Rome. If, on the other hand, he had told them not to pay the taxes, the Herodians would have accused him before Pilate as one who taught rebellion against the Roman government. The trap was well planned.

Questions concerning the dues of Caesar and the dues of God, the rights of the church and of the state, lawful civil claims and lawful spiritual claims, are hard knots which Christians have often found it difficult to untie, and almost impossible to solve. The cause of Christ always suffers when the devil succeeds in bringing churches into collisions and law-suits with the civil power. 'Give peace in our time, O Lord', is a prayer of wide meaning, and one that should often be on a Christian's lips.

Let us observe, in the last place, *the marvellous wisdom which our Lord showed in his answer to his enemies*. Their flattering words did not deceive him, for he knew 'their hypocrisy'. Saying to them, 'Bring me a denarius and let me look at it', he asked them, 'Whose likeness and inscription is this?' To which they were bound to reply, 'Caesar's'. They were themselves using a Roman coin, issued and circulated by the Roman government. As soon as they said this, Jesus silenced them by saying, 'Render to Caesar the things that are Caesar's, and to God the things that are God's.' He instructed them to pay tribute to the Roman government in temporal things, and to give obedience to God in spiritual things, and not to suppose that duty to an earthly sovereign and a heavenly sovereign are incapable of being reconciled to one another. In short, he tells the proud Pharisee not to refuse his dues to Caesar, and the worldly Herodian not to refuse his dues to God.

We learn from this the great principle that true Christianity was never intended to interfere with our obedience to civil powers. Rather, it ought to make us quiet, loyal and faithful subjects, who regard 'the governing authorities' as 'instituted by God' (Romans 13:1). If the law of the land and the law of God come into collision, there is no doubt that the Christian's course is clear: 'We must obey God rather than men' (Acts 5:39).

Let us pray for a larger measure of that spirit of wisdom which dwelt so abundantly in our Lord. Happy are those who remember Jesus' decision in this passage, understand it rightly, and make a practical application of it to their own times.

12:18–27

These verses relate a conversation between our Lord Jesus Christ and the Sadducees. The Sadducees taught 'that there is no resurrection'.

We learn here, *how much unfairness may often be detected in the arguments of those who lack true Christian faith*. The question put forward here by the Sadducees is a striking illustration of this. They told a tale of a woman who married seven brothers, one after the other, had no children, and outlived them all. They then asked Jesus, 'In the resurrection, when they rise again, whose wife will she be?' It rather appears as if they were making the story up, for it seems a very improbable one. But in that they were not interested. They desired only to raise a difficulty, and, if possible, to silence Jesus.

Three things are worth remembering, should we ever have cause to argue with such people as these. *First*, let us remember that they will invariably seek to press us with the difficult and obscure things of Christianity, and especially those things which are connected with the world to come. We must avoid this as far as possible, and seek (so far as we can) to turn the discussion to the great plain facts and evidences of the faith. *Second*, we must be on our guard against unfairness and dishonesty in argument. Many who challenge us have never studied the Bible which they pretend to deny, and have never calmly examined the foundations of the gospel. *Thirdly*, remember that every such questioner has a conscience, and to this we may appeal confidently. The very people who talk most loudly and disrespectfully against Christianity, often feel conscious (even while they talk) that they are wrong.

We learn, secondly, *how much of religious error may be traced to ignorance of the Bible*. Jesus' first words in reply to the Sadducees declare this plainly. He says, 'is this not the reason you are wrong, because you know neither the Scriptures nor the power of God?'

The truth of the principle here laid down, is proved by the facts in almost every age of church history. The reformation in Josiah's day was closely connected with the discovery of the book of the law. The false doctrines of the Jews in our Lord's time were the result of neglecting the Scriptures. The dark ages of the church were times when the Bible was held back from the people. The Protestant Reformation was mainly effected by translating and circulating the Bible. The churches which are most flourishing in our own day are churches which honour the Bible. The godliest families are Bible-reading families. The holiest men and women are Bible-reading people.

Let us not be ignorant of the Bible, lest we fall into some deadly error. Rather, let us read it diligently, and make it our rule of faith and practice. Let us labour to spread the Bible over the world, and teach our children to value it.

We learn, finally, *how different will be the state of things after the resurrection, from the state in which we live now.* Jesus tells us that 'when they rise from the dead, they neither marry nor are given in marriage, but are like angels in heaven'.

There are many difficulties connected with the life to come—not surprisingly, for the world beyond the grave is a world unseen by mortal eye, and therefore unknown. Even if we were told more, we should probably not understand it. What we do know is that the bodies of the saints will be raised, and—though glorified—will have a likeness to their bodies on earth, so that those who knew them once will know them again. And though raised with a real body, the risen saint will be freed completely from everything which is now an evidence of weakness and infirmity. So no more hunger or thirst, no more dying, no more weariness in serving God. Enjoying the full presence of God and of his Christ, men and women shall no longer need the marriage union, in order to help one another. We shall do his will perfectly and see his face continually.

There is comfort in all this for the true Christian. In the world to come, all will be changed. Nothing will be lacking to make our happiness complete. One thing only needs to be kept carefully in mind. Let us take heed that we rise again 'to the resurrection of life', and not to 'the resurrection of judgment' (John 5:29). To the believer in the Lord Jesus, the resurrection will be the greatest of blessings. To the worldly, the godless and the profane, the resurrection will be a misery and curse. Let us never rest until we are one with Christ, and Christ in us, and then we may look forward with joy to the life to come.

12:28–34

These verses contain a conversation between our Lord Jesus Christ and 'one of the scribes'. For the third time in a row we see Jesus tested with a hard question. Having silenced the Pharisees and Sadducees, he is now asked to decide a point upon which much difference of opinion prevailed among the Jews: 'Which commandment is the most important of all?' We have reason to bless God that so many hard questions were put to our Lord; little did these questioners think what benefit their questions would confer upon the Christian church, on account of the marvellous words of wisdom with which Jesus answered them.

Let us observe, in these verses, *how high is our Lord Jesus Christ's standard of duty to God and man*. The question which this scribe asked was a very wide one, and the answer he received was very likely not what he expected. He was certainly mistaken, if he thought that Jesus would commend to him the observance of some outward form or ceremony. He hears these solemn words: 'The Lord our God, the Lord is one. And you shall love the Lord your God with all your heart and with all your soul and with all your mind and with all your strength', and, 'You shall love your neighbour as yourself.'

How striking is Jesus' description of the *feeling* with which we ought to regard both God and our neighbour. We are not merely to obey the one, or to abstain from injuring the other; we are to give love, the strongest of all affections, and the most comprehensive. And how striking also is his description of the *measure* in which we should love God and neighbour. We are to love God with all the powers of our inward being, for we cannot love him too well. And we are to love our neighbour as ourselves, dealing with him in all respects as we would wish him to deal with us.

Let us keep these two grand rules continually before our minds, and use them daily in our journey through life. Let us see in them a summary of all that we should aim at in practice, both as regards God and man. Yet where are the men or women who can truthfully say that they have perfectly loved God and man? Where is the person on earth who must not plead 'guilty', when tried by such a law as this? No wonder that Scripture insists, 'None is righteous, no not one', and, 'For by works of the law no human being will be justified in his [God's] sight' (Romans 3:10, 20). How great is the need in which we all stand of the work of our Lord Jesus Christ upon the cross; how high needs to be our sense of the value of his shed blood for sinners.

Let us observe, for another thing, in these verses, *how far someone may go in religion, and yet not be a true disciple of Christ*. The scribe here was evidently a man of more knowledge than most of his equals, who saw things which many scribes and Pharisees never saw at all. His own words are a strong proof of this: 'You are right, Teacher. You have truly said that he [God] is one, and there is no other besides him. And to love him with all the heart and with all the understanding and with all the strength, and to love one's neighbour as oneself, is much more than all whole burnt offerings and sacrifices.' To which Jesus replied, 'You are not far from the kingdom of God.'

However, we must not shut our eyes to the fact that we are nowhere told that this man became one of Jesus' disciples. On this point there is a mournful silence. We are rather left to draw the painful conclusion that, like the rich young man, he could not make up his mind to give up all and follow Christ; or that, like the chief rulers mentioned elsewhere, he 'loved the glory that comes from man more than the glory that comes from God' (John 12:43). It may be that, though 'not far from the kingdom of God', he never entered it, and died outside it.

Cases like that of this scribe are, sadly, far from uncommon. There are so many who, like him, see much and know much of religious truth, and yet live and die undecided. So let us beware of resting our hopes of salvation on mere intellectual knowledge. We must not only know the leading doctrines of the gospel with our heads, but receive them into our hearts, and be guided by them in our lives. May we never rest until we are inside the kingdom of God, having truly repented, really believed, and having been made new creatures in Jesus Christ. If we remain satisfied with being 'not far from the kingdom', we shall find at last that we are shut out for evermore.

12:35–44

We have seen so far in this chapter how the enemies of our Lord endeavoured 'to trap him in his talk'. This present passage, however, begins with a question of a very different character, for it is Jesus himself who asks it. He asks his hearers about 'the Christ' and the meaning of Scripture.

Let us learn, firstly, *how much there is about Christ in the Old Testament Scriptures*. Jesus desires to expose the ignorance of the Jewish teachers about the true nature of the Messiah. He does so by referring to a passage in the Psalms, showing that the scribes did not understand it correctly. In so doing, he shows that David was inspired by the Holy Spirit to write about Christ.

We know from Jesus' words elsewhere that the Old Testament Scriptures 'bear witness about' him (John 5:39). They were intended to teach about Christ (by types, figures and prophecy) until he himself should appear on earth. Christ is undoubtedly to be found in every part of the law and the prophets, but very especially in the Psalms. His experience and sufferings at his first coming into the world, and his future glory and final triumph at his second coming, are the chief subjects of many a passage in that wonderful part of God's word.

Let us always beware of undervaluing or despising the Old Testament. There are probably many rich passages within it which have never yet been fully explored—deep things about Jesus in it, which many walk over like hidden gold mines, little knowing the treasures beneath their feet. Let us love *all* the Bible, for all is given by inspiration, and all is profitable. One part throws light upon another.

Let us learn, secondly, *how odious is the sin of hypocrisy in the sight of Christ*. This is a lesson taught by Jesus' warnings against the scribes. He exposes some of their practices—their showy manner of dressing, their love of the honour and praise of men rather than God, their love of money (disguised under a pretended concern for widows), and their long-winded public devotions (intended to make people think them eminently godly). And he concludes with the solemn declaration, 'They will receive the greater condemnation.'

Of all the sins into which men can fall, one of the worst is false profession and hypocrisy. This sin draws from Jesus' mouth strong language and heavy denunciations. It is bad enough to be led away captive by open sin; but it is even worse to pretend to be a true believer, while in reality we serve the world. Let us beware of falling into this sin. We cannot deceive an all-seeing God; 'God is not mocked'

(Galatians 6:7). He is a discerner of 'the thoughts and intentions of the heart' (Hebrews 4:12).

Let us show the world that there is true coin as well as counterfeit coin. Let us confess Christ modestly and humbly, but firmly and decidedly.

Let us learn, thirdly, *how pleasing to Christ is self-denying liberality in giving*. This lesson is taught in a striking manner, by Jesus' commendation of a certain poor widow. We are told that Jesus 'watched the people putting money into the offering box', and that 'Many rich people put in large sums'. Then he saw 'a poor widow' who 'out of her poverty has put in everything she had, all she had to live on'. Jesus then declared, 'Truly, I say to you, this poor woman has put in more than all who are contributing.' He looked not merely at the quantity contributed, but at the motive and heart of the contributor.

Let us ask God to stir up a spirit of liberality among his people. Above all, let each of us do our own duty, and give generously to Christian objects while we can. Let us give as those who remember that the eyes of Christ are upon us—he who sees exactly what each gives, and knows exactly how much is left behind. Most of all, let us give as the disciples of a crucified Saviour, who gave himself for us on the cross. We have received freely, so let us give freely.

Chapter 13

13:1–8

This chapter is full of prophecy—part of which has been fulfilled, and part remaining to be accomplished. Two great events form the subject of this prophecy. One is the destruction of Jerusalem, and the other is the second coming of our Lord Jesus Christ. The former was an event which happened only forty years after Jesus was crucified, while the latter is an event yet to come (and which we may yet live to see with our own eyes).

Chapters like these should be deeply interesting to every true Christian, for no history ought to receive so much of our attention as the past and future history of the church of Christ. The rise and fall of earthly empires are events of comparatively small importance in the sight of God. The march of armies and the victories of conquerors are mere trifles in comparison with the progress of the gospel and the final triumph of the 'Prince of Peace' (Isaiah 9:6).

Two things here demand our attention. The first is, *the prediction of our Lord concerning the temple at Jerusalem.* The disciples called their Master's attention to the architectural splendour of the temple: 'Look, Teacher, what wonderful stones and what wonderful buildings!' But they received from the Lord an answer very different from what they expected: 'Do you see these great buildings? There will not be left here one stone upon another that will not be thrown down.'

Let us learn from this solemn saying, that the true glory of a church does not consist in its buildings for public worship, but in the faith and godliness of its members. We are naturally inclined to judge things by the outward appearance, yet we are not to suppose that the Lord Jesus Christ can find pleasure in the most splendid places of worship among professing Christians, if his word and his Spirit are not honoured in it.

Yet let us not suppose, either, that it does not matter what kind of building is set apart for God's service. There is nothing to commend having a shabby or disorderly place of worship. 'But all things should be done decently and in order' (1 Corinthians 14:40). So let it be a settled principle for us, to regard pure doctrine and holy practice as the principal ornaments of a church. With these two things, the humblest brick cottage where the gospel is preached, is lovely and beautiful—for it is consecrated by Christ's own presence and the Holy Spirit's own blessing.

The second thing here demanding our attention is, *the remarkable manner in which our Lord commences the great prophecy of this chapter.* Four of Jesus' disciples (Peter, James, John and Andrew) 'asked him privately, "Tell us, when will these things be, and what will be the sign when all these things are about to be accomplished?"'

Jesus' answer to these questions begins at once with a prediction of coming false doctrine and coming wars. If the disciples thought Jesus would promise them immediate success and temporal prosperity in this world, they were soon corrected. Far from giving them to expect a speedy victory of truth, Jesus tells them to look out for the rise of error. 'See that no one leads you astray. Many will come in my name, saying, "I am he!"' And far from bidding them expect a general reign of peace and quietness, he tells them to prepare for wars and troubles. 'For nation will rise against nation, and kingdom against kingdom. There will be earthquakes in various places; there will be famines. These are but the beginning of the birth pains.'

These words of our Lord seem like the keynote of what his church is to expect between his first and second comings. We are not to indulge in extravagant expectations, imagining that the world will be converted before Jesus returns or that there will be a reign of peace. Yet let us wait patiently—let us labour, teach, work and pray.

13:9–13

In reading the prophecies in the Bible concerning Christ's church, we shall generally find judgment and mercy blended together—bitter with sweet, darkness with light. Jesus knows our weakness, and has taken care to mingle consolations with threatenings, kind words with hard words. This is evident in the prophecy here.

Observe, firstly, *what troubles our Lord bids his people expect between the time of his first and second comings*. Trouble is the portion of mankind, ever since Adam fell: 'man is born to trouble as the sparks fly upward' (Job 5:7). But there are special troubles to which believers in Jesus Christ are liable, and of these he gives clear warning here.

They must expect trouble *from the world*, not looking for help from 'governors and kings'. Christians will find that their ways and doctrines will bring them no favour in high places. On the contrary, they will often be imprisoned, beaten and put on trial—for no other reason than their adherence to the gospel of Christ.

They must expect trouble *from their own relations*. 'And brother will deliver brother over to death, and the father his child.' Christians' own flesh and blood may cease to love them, from hatred to their faith.

We do well to lay these things to heart, and to count the cost of being a Christian. We must be prepared to endure a measure of hardship, if we are real, thorough and decided Christians—we must be content to put up with laughter, ridicule, slander, and persecution—we must even bear hard words and unkindness from our nearest and dearest relations. The 'offence of the cross' (Galatians 5:11) has not ceased. 'The natural person does not accept the things of the Spirit of God' (1 Corinthians 2:14). If we are converted, we must never be surprised to experience the truth of Jesus' words, 'And you will be hated by all for my name's sake.'

Observe, secondly, *what rich encouragement the Lord Jesus holds out to his persecuted people*. He sets out here three rich cordials to cheer their souls.

He tells us that 'the gospel must first be proclaimed to all nations'. It must be, and it shall be. In spite of men and devils, the story of the cross of Christ shall be told in every part of the world. The word shall never be bound, though those who preach it may be imprisoned and put to death.

He tells us that those who are undergoing special trial for the gospel's sake shall have special help in their time of need. The Holy Spirit himself will assist them in making their defence, and they will be given a mouth and wisdom which their adversaries will not be able to gainsay or resist.

And he tells us that patient perseverance will result in final salvation. 'But the one who endures to the end will be saved.' Not one of those who endure tribulations shall miss his reward—all shall at length reap a rich harvest. 'Those who sow in tears shall reap with shouts of joy!' (Psalm 126:5).

Let us gather comfort from these precious promises for all true-hearted servants of Christ. We shall yet find ourselves on the victory side. We may be 'struck down, but not destroyed' (2 Corinthians 4:9). 'The kingdom of the world' will yet 'become the kingdom of our Lord and of his Christ, and he shall reign forever and ever' (Revelation 11:15). And when the scoffers and ungodly, who so often insulted them, are put to shame, believers shall 'receive the unfading crown of glory' (1 Peter 5:4).

13:14–23

We are taught in these verses, *the lawfulness of using means to provide for our own personal safety*. Jesus' language here is clear and unmistakable: 'let those who are in Judea flee to the mountains. Let the one who is on the housetop not go down, nor enter his house … and let the one who is in the field not turn back … Pray that it may not happen in winter'. Not a word is said to make us suppose that flight from danger, in certain circumstances, is unworthy of a Christian.

This lesson is one of wide application. A Christian is not to neglect the use of means, because he is a Christian, in the things of this life, any more than in the things of the life to come. Beyond doubt he may expect the special help of his Father in heaven, in every time of need; but he must expect it in the diligent use of lawful means.

The word of God contains several instructive examples on this subject, to which we shall do well to take heed. For example, there is the conduct of Jacob, when preparing to meet again with his brother Esau (Genesis 32–33), praying first, and then sending Esau a present—the conduct of Hezekiah, when Sennacherib came against Jerusalem (2 Chronicles 32)—and the conduct of Paul, who was often fleeing from place to place to preserve his life, and on one occasion was let down from the walls of Damascus in a basket (2 Corinthians 12:32–33).

Yet let us bear in mind one thing: let us not rest upon means while we use them, but look far beyond them to the blessing of God. To use all means diligently, and then leave the whole event in the hand of God, is the mark at which a true believer ought to aim.

We are also taught in these verses, *the great privileges of God's elect*. Twice the Lord uses a remarkable expression about them. He says, of these days of trouble, 'And if the Lord had not cut short the days, no human being would be saved. But for the sake of the elect, whom he chose, he shortened the days.' He says, of the 'False Christs and false prophets', that they 'will arise and perform signs and wonders, to lead astray, if possible, the elect'.

It is plain from this (and other passages in the Bible) that God has an elect people in the world, whom he has chosen in Christ 'before the foundation of the world' (Ephesians 1:4). To them, and only to them, belong the great privileges of justification, sanctification and final glory. To them belong the precious promises of the gospel. They are the bride, the Lamb's wife.

The subject of election is, without doubt, deep and mysterious—and it has often sadly been perverted and abused. But the misuse of truths must not prevent us from using them. Rightly used, election is a doctrine full of the sweetest comfort. That being so, however, election does not destroy man's responsibility and accountability. The great thing we have to do is to repent and believe the gospel—and we have no right to take any comfort from God's election unless we can show plain evidence of that repentance and faith. We are not to stand still, wondering anxiously whether we are elect or not, when God commands us plainly to repent and believe. To use the words of another Christian, we must begin at the *grammar school* of repentance and faith, before we go to the *university* of election.

13:24–31

This part of our Lord's prophecy on the Mount of Olives is entirely unfulfilled. Its events are yet to take place.

Observe, firstly, *what solemn majesty will attend our Lord Jesus Christ's second coming to this world.* The language used about the sun, moon and stars, conveys the idea of some universal convulsion at the close of this present age. It reminds us of Peter's words: 'and then the heavens will pass away with a roar, and the heavenly bodies will be burned up and dissolved' (2 Peter 3:10). At such a time as this, amid terror and confusion, men 'will see the Son of Man coming in clouds with great power and glory'.

The second coming of Christ will be utterly unlike the first. He came the first time in weakness, a tender infant, born of a poor woman in the manger at Bethlehem—unnoticed, unhonoured and scarcely known. He will come the second time in royal dignity, with the armies of heaven around him—to be known, recognised, and feared by all peoples of the earth. He came the first time to suffer, to bear our sins, to be made a curse—to be despised, rejected, unjustly condemned, and killed. He will come the second time to reign, to put down every enemy beneath his feet, to take the kingdoms of this world for his inheritance, to rule them with righteousness—to judge all men, and to live for evermore.

How vast the difference—how mighty the contrast—how startling the comparison between the two comings! Here are *comforting* thoughts for Christ's friends. Their own King will soon be here. They shall receive a rich reward for all that they have endured, and exchange a cross for a crown. Here are *confounding* words for Christ's foes. That same Jesus of Nazareth, whom they have so long despised and rejected, shall at last have the pre-eminence. That very Christ, whose gospel they have refused to believe, shall appear as their Judge, and (helpless, hopeless and speechless) they will have to stand before his bar. May we all lay these things to heart, and learn wisdom!

Observe, secondly, that *the first event after the Lord's coming shall be the gathering of his elect.* 'And then he will send out the angels and gather his elect from the four winds, from the ends of the earth to the ends of heaven.'

The safety of the Lord's people will be provided for, when judgment falls upon the earth. He will do nothing until he has placed them beyond the reach of harm. Just as the flood did not begin until Noah was safe in the ark, and the fire did not fall on Sodom until Lot was safe at Zoar—even so, the wrath of God on unbelievers will not be let loose until believers are hidden and secure. The true Christian may look forward to Christ's return without fear—for whatever terrible things shall come upon the earth, Jesus will take care that no harm comes to him.

Observe, thirdly, *how important it is to note the signs of our own times*. Jesus bids his disciples: 'From the fig tree learn its lesson.' Just as its budding leaves tell us that summer is near, so the fulfilment of events in the world around us should teach us that the Lord Jesus 'is near, at the very gates'. So it is fitting for all true Christians to observe carefully the public events of their own day. Our Lord rebukes the Jews for failing to 'interpret the signs of the times' (Matthew 16:3).

Observe, finally, *how carefully our Lord asserts the certainty of his predictions being fulfilled*. 'Heaven and earth will pass away, but my words will not pass away.' The words of Peter should never be forgotten: 'scoffers will come in the last days with scoffing, following their own sinful desires. They will say, "Where is the promise of his coming?"' (2 Peter 3:3–4).

Let us leave this passage with a thorough conviction of the truth of every part of its predictions, believing that every word of it shall prove at last to have been fully accomplished. Above all, let us make every effort to live under an abiding sense of its truth, like good servants ready to meet their master.

13:32–37

These words conclude Mark's report of our Lord's prophecy on the Mount of Olives. They ought to form a personal application of the whole discourse to our consciences.

We learn, first of all, from these verses, that *the exact time of our Lord Jesus Christ's second coming is purposely withheld from his church*. While the event is certain, the precise day and hour are not revealed. 'But concerning that day or that hour, no one knows, not even the angels in heaven, nor the Son, but only the Father.'

There is deep wisdom and mercy in this intentional silence. We have reason to thank God that the matter has been hidden from us—for uncertainty about the date of Jesus' return is calculated to keep believers in a state of constant expectation, and to preserve them from despondency. This very uncertainty supplies us with a reason for living always ready to meet him.

There is undoubtedly some difficulty in the words of our Lord that even he, the Son, does not know 'that day or that hour'. Since in him 'are hidden all the treasures of wisdom and knowledge' (Colossians 2:3), how can he be ignorant of anything? The answer is to be found in our lack of understanding of the great mystery of the union of two natures in one Person. That our Lord Jesus Christ was at the same time perfect God and perfect man, we know; and that these two distinct natures were both found together in his Person, we know. It must be enough for us to know that we sometimes see in our Lord's words and actions 'the man Christ Jesus' (1 Timothy 2:5), and sometimes 'the Christ who is God over all, blessed forever' (Romans 9:5). But though we see clearly, and admire, we cannot explain. We can only say that, in the present instance, our Lord spoke as a man, and not as God.

We learn, in the second place, from these verses, *what are the practical duties of all true believers in the prospect of the second coming of our Lord Jesus Christ.* Jesus mentions two things here, to which his people should attend. Given that he has told us that he is coming again one day in power and great glory, but that the precise date of that coming is not known—what are his people to do? How are we to live? We are to watch, and we are to work.

We are to *watch*. 'Be on guard, keep awake ... Therefore stay awake'. We are to be in a wakeful and lively state, prepared at any time to meet our Master—and avoiding all spiritual lethargy and dullness. 'So then let us not sleep, as others do, but let us keep awake and be sober' (1 Thessalonians 5:6). And we are to *work*. We are to realise that we are servants of a great Master, who has given to each one 'his work'. We are to labour to glorify God, each in our particular sphere, for there is always something for every one of the Lord's people to do. Our great desire must be to be found not idle and sleeping, but working and doing, when he returns.

Such are the simple instructions which our Lord sets before us. They ought to stir up in the hearts of all professing Christians great self-examination. Are we looking for our Saviour's return? Do we long for his appearing? Can we say with certainty, 'Come, Lord Jesus!' (Revelation 22:20)? Do we live as if we expected Christ to come again?

Chapter 14

14:1–9

This chapter begins that part of Mark's Gospel which describes our Lord's sufferings and death. So far, we have seen our Saviour chiefly as our prophet and teacher. Now we see him as our High Priest. Until now, we have considered his miracles and sayings. Now we are to consider his sacrifice on the cross.

Let us observe, first of all, *how God can disappoint the designs of wicked men, and overrule them to his own glory.* It is clear that Jesus' enemies did not intend to make his death a public occasion: 'And the chief priests and the scribes were seeking how to arrest him by stealth and kill him, for they said, "Not during the feast, lest there be an uproar from the people."' But the overruling providence of God completely defeated this design. Jesus' betrayal took place at an earlier time than the chief priests had expected, and his death took place on the very day when Jerusalem was most full of people, and the Passover feast was at its height. In every way, the counsel of these men was turned to foolishness. It is an easy thing for God to cause 'the wrath of man' to praise him (Psalm 76:10).

There is comfort in this for all true Christians. We live in a troubled world, and are often exercised anxiously about public events. Let us rest in the thought that everything is ordered for good by an all-wise God, and that all things in the world around us are working together for the Father's glory. Let us call to mind the words of the second psalm: 'The kings of the earth set themselves, and the rulers take counsel together, against the Lord and against his anointed'—which are then followed by: 'He who sits in the heavens laughs; the Lord holds them in derision' (Psalm 2:4). It has been so in time past, and it will be so in time to come.

Let us observe, secondly, *how good works are sometimes undervalued and misunderstood.* 'And while he (Jesus) was at Bethany in the house of Simon the leper, as he was reclining at table, a woman came with an alabaster flask of ointment of pure nard, very costly, and she broke the flask and poured it over his head.' She did this as a mark of honour and respect, and in token of her own gratitude and love towards him. Yet her act was blamed by some narrow-minded fault-finders, who accused her of waste and 'scolded her'.

There is never any shortage of those who denounce what they call 'extremes' in Christianity, and who recommend 'moderation' in the service of Christ. If someone devotes their time, money and affections to the pursuit of worldly things, they do not blame him. But if the same person devotes himself, and all that he has, to Christ, they find fault with him and call him a 'fanatic' or 'enthusiast'. Let us pity those who make such charges against believers, and not let the charges disturb us, if we hear them made against us because we seek to serve Christ. Once anyone understands the sinfulness of sin, and the mercy of Christ in dying for him, he will never think anything too good or too costly to be given to Christ. He will rather feel, 'What shall I render to the LORD for all his benefits to me?' (Psalm 116:12).

Let us observe, lastly, *how highly our Lord Jesus Christ esteems any service done to himself.* He bestows strong praises upon this woman. In particular, three things stand out in his words. For one thing, Jesus says, 'Why do you trouble her?' Then he says, 'She has done a beautiful thing to me.' And then he says, 'She has done what she could.'

Let us, like this devoted woman, devote ourselves, and all we have, to Christ's glory. Our position in the world may be lowly, and our means of usefulness few. But let us, like her, do what we can. And let us see here a sweet foretaste of things yet to come in the day of judgment. This same Jesus who pleaded the cause of his loving servant at Bethany, when she was blamed, will one day plead the cause of all who have been his servants in this world. Let us press on, remembering that his eye is upon us, and paying no heed to what men say or think of us. The praise of Christ at the last day, will more than compensate for all we suffer in this world from unkind tongues.

14:10–16

These verses record how Jesus was delivered into the hands of his enemies. This came to pass through the treachery of one his own twelve disciples. Judas Iscariot, the false apostle, betrayed him.

Mark, firstly, *to what lengths a man may go in a false profession of religion*. It is impossible to imagine a more striking proof of this painful truth, than the history of Judas Iscariot. He had looked like a true disciple of Jesus, and to be on his way to heaven. He was chosen by Jesus himself to be an apostle. He was privileged to be a companion of the Messiah, and an eye-witness of his mighty works, throughout Jesus' earthly ministry. He was sent forth to preach the kingdom of God, and to work miracles in Christ's name. It would seem that none of his fellow apostles suspected him of being a traitor. Yet this very man turned out to be false-hearted; he departed entirely from the faith and assisted our Lord's deadliest enemies. Never was there such a fall, such an apostasy, such a miserable end to a fair beginning—such a total eclipse of the soul.

How can this amazing conduct of Judas be accounted for? There is only one answer to that question—'the love of money' was the cause of this unhappy man's ruin. His act was one of covetousness; indeed, Scripture declares plainly that 'he was a thief' (John 12:6). His case stands before us as an eternal comment on the solemn words, 'For the love of money is a root of all kinds of evils' (1 Timothy 6:10).

Let us learn from this melancholy history of Judas, to be clothed 'with humility' (1 Peter 5:5), and to be content with nothing short of the grace of the Holy Spirit in our hearts. And let us 'guard against all covetousness' (Luke 12:15), and pray to 'be content with what (we) have' (Hebrews 13:5).

Mark, secondly, *the intentional connection between the time of the Jewish Passover and the time of Christ's death*. It was not by chance, but by God's providential appointment, that our Lord was crucified in the Passover week, and on the very day that the Passover lamb was slain. It was intended to draw the attention of the Jewish nation to Jesus as the true Lamb of God, and to bring to their minds the true object and purpose of his death. Every sacrifice, no doubt, pointed them to the one great sacrifice for sin which Christ was to offer. But none was so striking a figure and type of our Lord's sacrifice, as the slaying of the Passover lamb.

While the Passover was *a reminder* to the Jews of the marvellous deliverance of their forefathers out of the land of Egypt, when God slew the first-born—*a reminder* of the death then of an innocent lamb, which exempted them from the death of their own first-born—*a reminder* that the sprinkling of blood on the doorposts of the houses preserved them then from the sword of the destroying angel—and *a reminder* that no Jew then was safe unless he actually ate of the slain lamb—*it was far more than this*. It spoke of the *far greater* redemption and deliverance from the bondage of sin, which was brought in by the Lord Jesus Christ—of the *far higher* truth, that the death of Christ on the cross was to be the life of the world—of the *far more important* doctrine, that Christ's blood, sprinkled on man's conscience, cleanses it from all stain of guilt, and makes him safe from the wrath to come—and the *far higher* lesson, that all who would receive benefit from Christ's sacrifice must feed upon him by faith, and receive him into their hearts.

Let us call these things to mind and weigh them well. We shall then see a peculiar fitness and beauty in the time appointed by God for our Lord Jesus Christ's death on the cross. And let it be a rule with us, in our Bible reading, to study the Old Testament types with prayerful attention, for they are full of Christ. Matters such as the altar, the scapegoat, the daily burnt offering, the Day of Atonement—they are all so many finger-posts pointing to the great sacrifice offered by our Lord on Calvary. Those who examine these things with Christ as the key to their meaning, will find them full of gospel light and comfortable truth.

14:17–25

We have here Mark's account of the institution of the Lord's Supper. The simplicity of the description deserves special notice.

Let us learn from this passage, that *self-examination should precede the reception of the Lord's Supper*. We cannot doubt that this was one object of Jesus' solemn warning, 'Truly, I say to you, one of you will betray me, one who is eating with me.' He meant to stir up in the minds of his disciples those very searchings of heart which are here recorded—as well as to teach his whole church throughout the world, that the time of drawing near to the Lord's Table should be a time for diligent self-inquiry.

The benefit of the Lord's Supper depends entirely on the spirit and frame of mind in which we receive it. No good will be done to our souls, no blessing will be conveyed to us, by the bread which we there eat and the wine which we there drink, if we do not receive them rightly, worthily and with faith. Areas of self-examination should include these: Do we repent sincerely of our former sins? Do we purpose steadfastly to lead a new life? Have we a lively faith in God's mercy through Christ, and a thankful remembrance of his death? Are we in a right relationship with other people, and especially our Christian brothers and sisters?

Let us learn, in the second place, that *the principal object of the Lord's Supper is to remind us of Christ's sacrifice on the cross*. The bread is intended to bring to our recollection the body of Christ, which 'was wounded for our transgressions' (Isaiah 53:5). The wine is intended to bring to our recollection the blood of Christ, which was shed to cleanse 'us from all sin' (1 John 1:7). The false doctrine which some teach, that Jesus' death was nothing more than the death of a very holy man, who left us an example how to die, turns the Lord's Supper into a meaningless ordinance, and cannot possible be reconciled with our Lord's words at its institution.

A clear understanding of this will produce in us true *humility* of spirit, as we draw near to the Lord's Table. The bread and the wine will remind us how sinful sin must be, when nothing but Christ's death could atone for it. It will produce in us *hopefulness* about our souls. The bread and wine will remind us that though our sins are great, a great price has been paid for our redemption. Not least, it will produce in us *gratitude*. The bread and wine will remind us how great is our debt to Christ, and how deeply bound we are to glorify him in our lives. May these be the feelings we experience, whenever we receive the Lord's Supper!

Finally, let us learn from these verses, *the nature of the spiritual benefits which the Lord's Supper is intended to convey, and the persons who have a right to expect them*. We may gather this lesson from the significant actions which are used in receiving the bread and wine. Our Lord commands us to eat bread and to drink wine. Eating and drinking are acts of a living person, and the object of eating and drinking is to be strengthened and refreshed. From this, we may draw the conclusion that the Lord's Supper is intended for the strengthening and refreshing of our souls, and that those who ought to partake of it are those who are living, real Christians.

So the Lord's Supper is for believers, and not for unbelievers, for the living and not for the dead. It is intended to sustain life, not to impart it—to strengthen and increase grace, but not to give it—to help faith to grow, but not to sow or plant it. It will assist true Christians to rest in Christ more simply, and to trust in him more entirely. It will aid, quicken and confirm their faith.

14:26–31

We see in these verses, *how well our Lord foreknew the weakness and infirmity of his disciples*. He tells them plainly what they were going to do: 'You will all fall away.' He tells Peter in particular of the astounding sin which he was about to commit: 'Truly, I tell you, this very night, before the rooster crows twice, you will deny me three times.'

Yet Jesus' foreknowledge did not prevent him from choosing these twelve disciples to be his apostles. He allowed them to be his intimate friends and companions, knowing perfectly well what they would one day do. So let us take comfort in the thought that the Lord Jesus does not cast off his believing people because of failures and imperfections. He knows what they are, and takes them with all their blemishes and defects, and, once joined to him by faith, will never put them away. It is his glory to pass over the transgressions of his people, and to cover their sins—both from before their conversions, and since. He loved them then, and he loves them still. He has undertaken to save them, notwithstanding all their shortcomings, and what he has undertaken he will perform.

The church of Christ is rather like a great hospital; we are all, more or less, weak, and all daily in need of the skilful treatment of the heavenly Physician. So let us learn to pass a charitable judgment on the conduct of professing believers, not saying they have no grace because we see in them much weakness and corruption. Let us remember that our Master in heaven bears with their infirmities, and let us try to bear with them too. There will be no complete cures until the resurrection day.

We see, secondly, *how much comfort professing Christians may miss by carelessness and inattention.* Jesus spoke plainly of his resurrection: 'But after I am raised up, I will go before you to Galilee.' Yet not one of the disciples seems to have grasped these words, or treasured them up in their hearts. When Jesus was betrayed, they forsook him; when he was crucified, they were almost in despair; and when he rose again on the third day, they would not believe that it was true.

What an exact picture we have here of human nature. How often we see the very same thing among professing Christians. How many truths we read, year by year, in the Bible, and yet remember them no more than if we had never read them at all. How many words of wisdom we hear in sermons, yet live on as if we had never heard them. Then, when days of darkness and affliction come upon us in due course, we prove unarmed and unprepared.

Let us pray for a quick understanding in reading and hearing God's word, searching into every part of it, so as not to lose any precious truth in it for lack of care. And let ministers be patient; even if their preaching often seems to pass unnoticed and unheeded, yet truths that seem to have been neglected at first often bear fruit after many days.

We see, finally, *how much ignorant self-confidence may sometimes be found in the hearts of professing Christians.* Peter could not think it possible that he could ever deny his Lord, and said to Jesus: 'Even though they all fall away, I will not ... If I must die with you, I will not deny you.' And he did not stand alone in his confidence. The other disciples were of the same opinion: 'And they all said the same.' Yet what did this confident boasting come to? Only a few hours passed before they forsook him and fled. Their loud professions were all forgotten. So little do we know how we shall act in any particular situation until we are placed in it.

We need to pray for humility. 'Pride goes before destruction, and a haughty spirit before a fall' (Proverbs 16:18). We never can tell how far we might fall, if once placed in temptation. There is no degree of sin into which the greatest saint may not run, if he is not upheld by the grace of

God, and if he does not watch and pray. 'Therefore let anyone who thinks that he stands take heed lest he fall' (1 Corinthians 10:12). Let our daily prayer be: 'Hold me up, that I may be safe' (Psalm 119:117).

14:32–42

The history of our Lord's agony in the garden of Gethsemane is a deep and mysterious passage of Scripture. Yet it has upon its surface plain truths of most momentous importance.

Note, firstly, *how keenly our Lord felt the burden of the world's sin*. We are told that he 'began to be greatly distressed and troubled. And he said to them, 'My soul is very sorrowful, even to death''—and that 'he fell on the ground and prayed that, if it were possible, the hour might pass from him'.

There is only one reasonable explanation of these expressions. He spoke, not from mere fear of the physical suffering of death, but from a sense of the enormous load of human guilt, which began at that time to press upon him in a peculiar manner. It was a sense of the unutterable weight of our sins and transgressions which were then especially laid upon him.

How this shows us the exceeding sinfulness of sin. Let the recollection of Gethsemane have a sanctifying effect upon us.

Note, secondly, *what an example our Lord gives us of the importance of prayer in time of trouble*. In the hour of his distress, twice we are told that he prayed.

We shall never find a richer encouragement than this for the patient bearing of affliction. The first person to whom we should turn in trouble is God. The reply may not be given immediately, nor the relief we request be granted at once. Indeed, the matter that tries us may never be removed. But the mere act of pouring out our hearts at the throne of grace will be a blessing to us. The advice of James is wise and weighty: 'Is anyone among you suffering? Let him pray' (James 5:13).

Note, thirdly, *what a striking example our Lord gives us of submission of will to the will of God*. Deeply as his human nature felt the pressure of a world's guilt, he still prays, 'if it were possible, the hour might pass from him. And he said, "Abba, Father, all things are possible for you. Remove this cup from me. Yet not what I will, but what you will."'

We cannot imagine any higher degree of perfection than that which is set before us here. To take patiently whatever God sends—to like nothing but what God likes—to wish nothing but what God approves—to prefer pain, if it please God to send it, to ease, if God does not think fit to bestow it—to lie passive under God's hand, and know no will but his—this is the highest standard at which we can aim, and of this our Lord's conduct in Gethsemane is the perfect pattern.

Note, finally, *how much infirmity may be found even in the best Christians*. We have a painful illustration of this truth in the conduct of Peter, James and John. They slept when they ought to have watched and prayed. Though invited by Jesus to watch with him—though warned a short time before that danger was at hand and their faith likely to fail—though fresh from the last supper, they slept.

These things are written for our learning. Let us take heed that they are not written in vain. The best of men are but men, and as long as saints are in the body, they are compassed with infirmity. Jesus' solemn counsel to us is this: 'Watch and pray that you may not enter into temptation.' It should be the Christian's motto from the time of his conversion to the hour of his death. Whenever we feel the spirit of sloth or laziness coming upon us (and especially in the matter of our private prayers) let us remember Peter, James and John in the garden, and take care.

We must watch like soldiers, for we are upon enemy's ground and must always be on our guard. We must fight a daily fight and war a daily warfare. The Christian's rest is yet to come. We must pray without ceasing—regularly, habitually, carefully. We must pray as well as watch, and watch as well as pray. The one who knows his own weakness, and knowing it both watches and prays, is the one who will be held up and not allowed to fall.

14:43–52

Let us notice here, *how little our Lord's enemies understood the nature of his kingdom*. We read that 'Judas came, one of the twelve, and with him a crowd with swords and clubs, from the chief priests and the scribes and the elders.' It was evidently expected that Jesus would be defended vigorously by his disciples, and that he had would not be taken prisoner without fighting. These religious leaders clung obstinately to the idea that our Lord's kingdom was a worldly kingdom, and therefore supposed that it would be upheld by worldly means. They had yet to learn the solemn lesson contained in Jesus' words to Pilate: 'My kingdom is not of this world' (John 18:36).

The cause of truth does not need force to maintain it. 'For the weapons of our warfare are not of the flesh' (2 Corinthians 10:4). The gospel of Christ stands by the power of the Holy Spirit. It grows by the hidden influence of the Holy Spirit upon men's hearts and consciences. 'Not by might, nor by power, but by my Spirit, says the LORD of hosts' (Zechariah 4:6).

Let us notice, secondly, *how all things in our Lord's passion happened according to God's word*. His own address to those who arrested him, exhibits this in a striking manner: 'But let the Scriptures be fulfilled.'

There was neither accident nor chance in any part of the close of Jesus' earthly ministry. The steps in which he walked from Gethsemane to Calvary were all marked out hundreds of years before. Psalm 22 and Isaiah 53 were literally fulfilled. All that took place was only the working out of God's great designs. The wrath of Jesus' enemies, his rejection by his own people, his being dealt with as a criminal, his being condemned by the assembly of the wicked—all had been foreknown, and all foretold. The armed men whom Judas brought to take hold of Jesus, were unconscious instruments in carrying God's purposes into effect.

Let us rest our souls on the thought that all around us is ordered and overruled by God's almighty wisdom—in both the course of the world and the position of the church. There is a hand above us, moving the vast machine of the universe, and making all things work together for his glory. The Scriptures are constantly being fulfilled.

Let us notice, lastly, *how much the faith of true believers may give way*. We learn that when Judas and his company laid hands on our Lord, and he quietly submitted to being taken prisoner, 'they (the disciples) all left him and fled'. The fear of present danger got the better of faith. The sense of immediate peril drove every other feeling from their minds.

Let us learn from this, not to be over-confident in our own strength. The fear of man does indeed bring a snare. We never know what we may do, if we are tempted, or to what extent our faith may give way. Let us be clothed with humility—and, also, charitable in our judgment of other Christians. Let us never forget that even our Lord's chosen apostles forsook him in his time of need—yet they rose again by repentance, and became pillars of the church of Christ.

And let us leave this passage with a deep sense of our Lord's ability to sympathise with his believing people. If there is one trial greater than another, it is the trial of being disappointed in those we love. It is a bitter cup, which all true Christians have frequently to drink. But take comfort in the thought, that there is one unfailing Friend, even Jesus, who can be touched with the feeling of our infirmities, and has tasted all of our sorrows. He knows what it is to see friends and disciples failing him in the hour of need. Yet he bore it patiently, and loved them notwithstanding. He is never weary of forgiving—and let us seek to do likewise.

14:53–65

We read in Ecclesiastes 10:6 of when 'folly is set in many high places, and the rich sit in a low place'. A complete illustration of this is given in the state of things recorded in this passage. We see the Son of God brought before 'all the chief priests and the elders and the scribes'. The heads of the Jewish nation combined together to kill their own Messiah, and to judge him who will one day come in glory to judge them and all mankind.

Observe, firstly, *how foolishly Christians sometimes thrust themselves into temptation.* We are told that when our Lord was led away prisoner, 'Peter had followed him at a distance, right into the courtyard of the high priest. And he was sitting with the guards and warming himself at the fire'. This was not a wise thing for him to do. Having already once forsaken his Master and fled, he ought to have remembered his own weakness, and not to have ventured into danger again. It brought on him fresh trials of faith, for which he was utterly unprepared, and paved the way for his greatest transgression: his thrice-repeated denial of Jesus.

Once a believer has begun to backslide and leave his first faith, he seldom stops short at his first mistake, or makes only one stumble, or commits only one fault. Like a stone rolling downhill, the further he goes on in sinning, the faster and more decided is his course. So if we know anything of truly being saved, let us constantly beware of the beginnings of backsliding. It is like the letting out of water—first a drop and then a torrent. Once out of the way of holiness, there is no saying to what we may come. Let us not play with fire. Let us never fear being too particular, too strict, or too precise. Our humble prayer must ever be, 'lead us not into temptation' (Matthew 6:13).

Observe, secondly, *how much our Lord Jesus Christ had to endure from lying lips, when tried before the chief priests*. 'For many bore false witness against him, but their testimony did not agree.'

This must have been one of the heaviest parts of our blessed Saviour's passion. To be seized unjustly as a criminal and put on trial as a criminal when innocent, with men inventing false charges, is a severe affliction. Yet this was all part of the cup which Jesus drank for our sakes. Great indeed was the price at which our souls were redeemed.

Let it never surprise true Christians if they are slandered and misrepresented in this world. They must not expect to fare better than their Lord. Let them rather look forward to it as a matter of course, and see in it a part of the cross which all must bear after conversion. Lies and false reports are among Satan's regular weapons. Jesus' words should often come to our minds: 'Woe to you, when all people speak well of you' (Luke 6:16)—and, 'Blessed are you when others revile you and persecute you and utter all kinds of evil against you falsely on my account' (Matthew 5:11).

Observe, finally, *what distinct testimony our Lord bore to his own Messiahship and second coming in glory*. The high priest asked Jesus the solemn question, 'Are you the Christ, the Son of the Blessed?' Immediately, he received the emphatic reply from Jesus, 'I am, and you will see the Son of Man seated at the right hand of Power, and coming with the clouds of heaven.'

The Jews could never say after these words, that they were not told clearly that Jesus of Nazareth was the Christ of God, or say that he was not worthy to be believed. He warned them plainly that his glory and greatness was all yet to come. They would see him, in due time, coming as Judge, Conqueror and King. If Israel was unbelieving, it was not because Israel was not told what to believe.

Let us leave this passage with a deep sense of the reality and certainty of our Lord Jesus Christ's second coming. Let us live in the daily recollection that our Saviour is one day coming back—that the Christ in whom we believe is not only the Christ who died and rose again, and the Christ who lives and intercedes for us, but the Christ who will return in glory, to gather together and reward his people, and to punish fearfully all his enemies.

14:66–72

A shipwreck is a melancholy sight, even when no lives are lost. Yet no shipwreck is half so melancholy a sight as the backsliding and fall of a true Christian. Though raised again by God's mercy, and finally saved from hell, he loses much by his fall. Such a sight is now brought before us in these verses, where we are given the painful and instructive account of how Peter denied his Lord.

Learn, first of all, *how far and how shamefully a great saint may fall*. We know that Simon Peter was an eminent apostle of Jesus Christ. He was one who had received special commendation from our Lord's lips, after his noble confession of Jesus' Messiahship. He was one who had enjoyed special privileges, and had special mercies shown to him. Yet here we see this same Simon Peter so entirely overcome by fear that he actually denies his Lord—and he does it not only once, but three times, and even with cursing and swearing. He declares that he did not know him whom he had accompanied for three years—the one who had healed his own mother-in-law, taken him up onto the mount of transfiguration, and saved him from drowning in the Sea of Galilee. And, above all, he did this in the face of the plainest warnings he had received, and of his own loud protestations that he would rather die than ever do such a thing.

These things are written to show the church of Christ what human nature is, even in the best of men—and that, even after conversion, believers are compassed with infirmity and liable to fall. They impress upon us the immense importance of daily watchfulness, prayerfulness, and humility. And let us remember that Peter's case does not stand alone—the histories of Noah, Abraham, David, and Hezekiah supply us with further examples of the infirmity of true believers. So let us learn 'to walk humbly with (our) God' (Micah 6:8).

Learn, secondly, *how small a temptation may cause a saint to have a great fall.* The beginning of Peter's experience here was nothing more than the simple remark of 'one of the servant girls of the high priest', who said to him, 'You also were with the Nazarene, Jesus.' There is no indication that she spoke with any hostile purpose. Yet this simple remark was enough to overthrow the faith of an eminent apostle, and to make him begin to deny his Master.

This ought to teach us that no temptation is too small and trifling to overcome us, unless we watch and pray to be upheld. If God be for us, we may remove mountains and get the victory over a host of foes; but if God withdraws his grace, and leaves us to ourselves, we are like a city without gates and walls, a prey to the first enemy.

So let us beware of making light of temptations because they seem little or insignificant. There is nothing little where our souls are concerned. A little leaven leavens the whole lump—a little spark may kindle a great fire—a little leak may sink a great ship—and a little provocation may bring out from our hearts great corruption, and end in bringing our souls into great trouble.

Learn, finally, *that backsliding brings saints into great sorrow.* The conclusion of this passage is very moving. 'And Peter remembered how Jesus had said to him, "Before the rooster crows twice, you will deny me three times."' Who can pretend to describe the feelings that must have flashed across the apostle's mind—the shame, confusion, self-reproach, and bitter remorse which must have overwhelmed his soul? There is deep and solemn meaning in the words, 'And he broke down and wept.'

Let us leave this passage with the settled conviction that sin is sure to lead to sorrow, and that the way of most holiness is always the way of most happiness. It will never profit the Lord's servants to walk carelessly and to give way to temptation. If we turn our backs on the Lord Jesus, we shall be sure to feel the pain of it. Though he forgives us, he will make us feel the folly of our ways. Those who follow the Lord most fully, will always follow him most comfortably.

Chapter 15

15:1–15

These verses begin the chapter in which Mark describes the slaying of 'the Lamb of God, who takes away the sin of the world!' (John 1:29). It is a part of the gospel history which should always be read with peculiar reverence. We should call to mind that Christ was cut off, not for himself, but for us (Daniel 9:26)—that his death is the life of our souls, and that unless his blood had been shed, we must have perished miserably in our sins.

Let us mark in these verses, *what a striking proof the Jewish rulers gave to their own nation that the times of Messiah had come*. The chapter opens with the fact that 'the chief priests held a consultation with the elders and scribes and the whole Council. And they bound Jesus and led him away and delivered him over to Pilate', the Roman governor. Why did they do this? Because they no longer had the power of putting anyone to death, and were under the dominion of the Romans.

Prophecy was being fulfilled, yet their eyes were blinded. Their conduct was long ago foreseen and foretold, yet they either could not, or would not, see what they were doing. In the very height of their madness, folly and unbelief, they pressed on, to their own ruin.

Let us mark, secondly, in these verses, *the meekness and lowliness of our Lord Jesus Christ*. When he stood before Pilate and 'the chief priests accused him of many things', he 'made no answer'. Although the charges against him were false, and he knew no sin, he was content to endure the hostility of sinners against himself (Hebrews 12:3), saying nothing. Though he was innocent of any transgression, he submitted to bear groundless accusations made against him, without a murmur. Great is the contrast between the second Adam and the first. Our first father, Adam, was guilty, and yet tried to excuse himself. The second Adam, Jesus, was guiltless, yet made no defence at all. As it is put in Isaiah 53:7, 'like a lamb that is led to the slaughter, and like a sheep that before its shearers is silent, so he opened not his mouth'.

Here is a practical lesson for us to learn from our Saviour's example: to suffer patiently, and not to complain, whatever God may think fit to lay upon us. Nothing in the Christian character glorifies God so much as patient suffering. 'But if when you do good and suffer for it you endure, this is a gracious thing in the sight of God. For to this you have been called, because Christ also suffered for you, leaving you an example, so that you might follow in his steps' (1 Peter 2:20–21).

Let us mark, thirdly, in these verses, *the wavering and undecided conduct of Pilate*. It is clear that Pilate was convinced of our Lord's innocence. 'For he perceived that it was out of envy that the chief priests had delivered him up.' We see Pilate struggling for a time to obtain Jesus' acquittal, and to satisfy his own conscience. At last he yields to the persistence of the Jews, and, 'wishing to satisfy the crowd', delivers Jesus to be crucified.

A man in high place without religious principles is one of the most pitiable sights in the world. He is like a large ship tossed to and fro on the sea without compass or rudder. His very position surrounds him with temptations and snares, and gives him power for good or evil. Let us pray much for great men and not envy them, for they need great grace to keep them from the devil. High places are slippery places. 'And do you seek great things for yourself? Seek them not' (Jeremiah 45:5).

Let us mark, fourthly, in these verses, *the exceeding guilt of the Jews in the matter of the death of Christ*. At the eleventh hour the chief priests had an opportunity of repenting, if they would have taken it. They were given the choice of whether Jesus or Barabbas should be allowed to go free. They chose to give a murderer his freedom, and to have 'the Author of life' (Acts 3:15) put to death. The *power* of putting our Lord to death was no longer theirs—the *responsibility* of his death they publicly took upon themselves. To Pilate's question to them, 'Then what shall I do with the man you call the King of the Jews?', they responded, 'Crucify him.'

To reject Christ and choose Barabbas was indeed an astounding act. But let us be careful not to follow the example of the Jews here, lest we too, at the last, are found to have made the same choice. The service of sin and the service of God are continually before us. The friendship of the world and the friendship of Christ are continually pressed upon our notice. Are we making the right choice? Are we cleaving to the right Friend? These are solemn questions; happy is the one who can give them a satisfactory answer.

Let us mark, finally, in these verses, *what a striking type the release of Barabbas provides of the gospel plan of salvation*. The guilty is set free, and the innocent is put to death. The great sinner is delivered, and the sinless one remains bound. Barabbas is spared, and Christ is crucified.

We have in this striking fact a vivid emblem of the manner in which God pardons and justifies the ungodly. He does it, because Christ has suffered in their place, 'the righteous for the unrighteous' (1 Peter 3:18). They deserve punishment, but a mighty Substitute has suffered for them; they deserve eternal death, but a glorious Surety has died for them. We were all by nature in the position of Barabbas—guilty, wicked, worthy of condemnation. But when we were without hope, Christ the innocent died for the ungodly. And now God, for Christ's sake, can be 'just and the justifier of the one who has faith in Jesus' (Romans 3:26).

Let us bless God that we have such a glorious salvation set before us. Our plea must always be—not that we are deserving of acquittal, but that Christ has died for us. Let us take heed that, having 'such a great salvation' (Hebrews 2:3), we really make use of it for our own souls—never resting until we can say by faith, 'Christ is mine. I deserve hell. But Christ has died for me, and believing in him I have a hope of heaven.'

15:16–32

This passage is one of those which shows us the infinite love of Christ towards sinners. When we reflect that the sufferer here was the eternal Son of God, we are lost in wonder and amazement. And when we reflect further that these sufferings were voluntarily endured to deliver sinful men and women like ourselves from hell, we may see something of Paul's meaning, when he speaks of 'the love of Christ that surpasses knowledge' (Ephesians 3:19)—and again, 'but God shows his love for us in that while we were still sinners, Christ died for us' (Romans 5:8).

Let us follow Jesus' passion step by step from the moment of his condemnation by Pilate to his last hour on the cross. Remember, it is the death of our own Surety and Substitute that we are reading.

First of all, *we see Jesus delivered into the hands of the Roman soldiers, as a criminal condemned to death.* He before whom the whole world will one day stand and be judged, allowed himself to be sentenced unjustly, and given over into the hands of wicked men. *And why was this?* It was that we, the poor sinful children of men, believing on him, might be delivered from the pit of destruction and the torment of the prison of hell. It was that we might be set free from every charge in the day of judgment, and be presented 'blameless before the presence of (God's) glory with great joy' (Jude 24).

Secondly, *we see Jesus insulted and made a laughing-stock by the Roman soldiers.* 'And they clothed him in a purple cloak', in derision, 'and twisting together a crown of thorns, they put it on him', in mockery of his kingdom. 'And they were striking his head with a reed and spitting on him', as one utterly contemptible. *And why was this?* It was that we, vile as we are, might have glory, honour and eternal life through faith in Christ's work on the cross. It was that we might be received into God's kingdom with triumph at the last day, and 'receive the unfading crown of glory' (1 Peter 5:4).

Thirdly, *we see Jesus stripped of his garments and crucified before his enemies.* The soldiers who led him away, 'divided his garments among them, casting lots for them'. *And why was this?* It was that we, who have no righteousness of our own, might be clothed in the perfect righteousness that Christ has wrought out for us, and not stand naked before God at the last day. It was done, that we, who are all defiled with sin, might have a wedding garment, in which we may sit down by the side of angels, and not be ashamed.

Fourthly, *we see Jesus suffering the most shameful and humiliating of all deaths, 'even death on a cross'* (Philippians 2:8). It was the punishment reserved for the worst of criminals. The man on whom it was inflicted was counted accursed—'for it is written, "Cursed is everyone who is hanged on a tree"' (Galatians 3:13). *And why was this?* It was that we, who are born in sin and children of wrath, might be counted blessed for Christ's sake. It was done to remove the curse we all deserve because of sin, by laying it on Christ. 'Christ redeemed us from the curse of the law by becoming a curse for us' (Galatians 3:13).

Fifthly, *we see Jesus reckoned a transgressor and sinner*. 'And with him they crucified two robbers, one on his right and one on his left.' He who had done no sin, 'was numbered with the transgressors' (Isaiah 53:12). *And why was this?* It was that we, who are miserable transgressors, both by nature and practice, may be reckoned innocent for Christ's sake. It was done that we, who are worthy of nothing but condemnation, may be counted worthy to escape God's judgment, and be pronounced not guilty before the assembled world.

Lastly, *we see Jesus mocked when dying, as one who was an impostor, and unable to save himself. And why was this?* It was that we, in our last hours, through faith in Christ may have strong consolation. It all came to pass that we may enjoy a strong assurance, may 'know whom (we) have believed' (2 Timothy 1:12), and may go 'through the valley of the shadow of death' (Psalm 23:4) fearing no evil.

Let us leave this passage with a deep sense of the enormous debt which all believers owe to Christ. All that they have, are and hope for, may be traced to the doing and dying of the Son of God. Through his condemnation, they have acquittal—through his sufferings, peace—through his shame, glory—through his death, life. Their sins were imputed to him, and his righteousness is imputed to them. No wonder Paul declares, 'Thanks be to God for his inexpressible gift!' (2 Corinthians 9:15).

And let us also leave this passage with the deepest sense of Christ's unutterable love to our souls. What are we? We are corrupt, evil and miserable sinners. Who is he? He is the eternal Son of God, the maker of all things. Yet, for our sakes, he endured the most painful, horrible and disgraceful death. Surely the thought of this love should compel us daily to live not to ourselves, but to Christ. It should make us ready 'to present (our) bodies as a living sacrifice' (Romans 12:1) to him who lived and died for us.

15:33–38

These verses record the death of our Lord Jesus Christ. All deaths are solemn events—nothing in the whole history of a man is so important as his end. But never was there a death of such solemn moment as that which is now before us. In the instant that Jesus drew his last breath, the work of atonement for sin was accomplished. The ransom for sinners was paid, and the kingdom of heaven was thrown fully open to all believers.

Observe here, firstly, *the visible signs and wonders which accompanied our Lord's death*. Mark mentions two in particular: the darkening of the sun for three hours, and the tearing of the curtain which divided the holy of holies from the holy place in the temple. Both were miraculous events, both had a deep meaning about them, and both were calculated to arrest the attention of the whole multitude assembled at Jerusalem.

What did the miraculous darkness teach? It taught the exceeding wickedness of the Jewish nation, who were actually crucifying their own Messiah and slaying their own King. The sun itself hid its face at the sight. And it taught the exceeding sinfulness of sin in the eyes of God. The Son of God was left without the cheering light of day, when he was made sin for us and carried our transgressions.

What did the miraculous tearing of the temple curtain mean? It taught the abolition and termination of the whole Jewish ceremonial law. It taught that the way into the holiest of all was now thrown open to all mankind by Christ's death. It taught that Gentiles as well as Jews might now draw near to God with boldness, through Jesus the one High Priest, and that all barriers between man and God were for ever cast down.

Observe here, secondly, *how truly and really our Lord Jesus Christ was made a curse for us, and bore our sins*. It is brought out strikingly in the words which he used from Psalm 22:1, 'My God, my God, why have you forsaken me?'

We cannot pretend to fathom all the depth of meaning which these words contain. They imply an amount of mental suffering, such as we are unable to conceive. The agony of some of God's holiest servants has been on occasions very great, under an impression of God's favour being withdrawn from them. What then may we suppose was the agony of the holy Son of God—when all the sin of the world was laid upon his head, when he felt himself reckoned guilty though without sin, when he felt his Father's countenance turned away from him?

This dying cry is utterly unintelligible without the mighty scriptural doctrine of Jesus' substitution on the cross for sinners. If he was only a mere man, or if his death be reduced to a great example of self-sacrifice, it cannot be accounted for. The truth is, that he uttered his dying cry under the heavy pressure of a world's sin laid upon him, and charged to him.

Observe here, lastly, *that it is possible to be forsaken by God for a time, and yet to be loved by him*. Although we hear Jesus saying to his Father, 'why have you forsaken me?', he addresses God as 'My God'. We know, also, that our Lord was only forsaken for a season, and that even when forsaken he was the beloved Son in whom (both in his suffering and doing) the Father was well pleased.

Without doubt there is a sense in which our Lord's feeling of being 'forsaken' was peculiar to himself, since he was suffering for our sins and not for his own. Even so, however, there remains this great fact that Jesus, who was for a time forsaken by the Father, was for all that time still the Father's beloved Son. As it was with the great head of the church, so it may be in a modified sense with his members. They too—though chosen and beloved of the Father—may sometimes feel God's face turned away from them (maybe in times of illness or affliction, or from carelessness in our walk, or because God would draw us nearer to himself).

At such times, believers need to learn from our Lord's experience, not give way to despair, and search their own hearts. But let them not conclude hastily that they are cast off for ever, are self-deceivers, or that they have no grace at all. Let them still wait on the Lord, and say with Job, 'Though he slay me, I will hope in him' (Job 13:15). Let them remember also the words of Isaiah 50:10 and Psalm 42:11—'Let him who walks in darkness and has no light trust in the name of the LORD and rely on his God'—'Why are you cast down, O my soul, and why are you in turmoil within me? Hope in God; for I shall again praise him, my salvation and my God.'

15:39–47

The death of our Lord Jesus Christ is the most important fact in Christianity. On it depend the hopes of all saved sinners both for time and eternity. We need not be surprised, therefore, to find the reality of Jesus' death carefully placed beyond dispute. Three kinds of witnesses to the fact are brought before us in these verses: the Roman centurion who stood near the cross, the women who followed our Lord from Galilee to Jerusalem, and the disciples who buried him. Their united evidence is above suspicion. Our Saviour truly and really died.

Notice, for one thing, *what honourable mention is made here of women*. When Jesus died, 'There were also women looking on from a distance.' The names of some of them are recorded. We are told that when Jesus 'was in Galilee, they followed him and ministered to him', and that 'there were also many other women who came up with him to Jerusalem'.

It is interesting to remark how often through the New Testament we find the grace of God glorified in women, and how much benefit God has been pleased to confer through them on the church, and on the world. We see Jesus born of a woman, and life and immortality brought to light by that miraculous event. We see women mentioned as a help and assistance to the cause of the gospel (such as Elizabeth, Mary, Martha, Dorcas, Lydia, Phoebe, and others). There is a great work that women can do for God's glory, without them being public teachers. Happy is that congregation where women know this, and act upon it!

Notice, for another thing, *that Jesus has friends of whom little is known*. A remarkable proof of this is someone who is mentioned here for the first time: Joseph of Arimathea. We do not know how he had come to love Christ and to desire to do him honour; and we know nothing of his subsequent history after what is recorded of him here. What we are told is that he 'was also himself looking for the kingdom of God'. At a time when Jesus' disciples had forsaken him, Joseph 'took courage and went to Pilate and asked for the body of Jesus'. He then 'laid him in a tomb'. Others had shown love to Jesus while he was speaking and living, but Joseph showed love to him when he was silent and dead.

There are true Christians on earth, of whom we know nothing, and in places where we might not expect to find them. The Lord has many 'hidden ones' in his church, who—unless brought forward by special circumstances—will never be known until the last day. The words of God to Elijah should not be forgotten: 'Yet I will leave seven thousand in Israel' (1 Kings 19:18).

Notice, lastly, *what honour our Lord Jesus Christ has placed on the grave, by allowing himself to be laid in it.* We read that Jesus was laid 'in a tomb that had been cut out of the rock', and that a stone was rolled 'against the entrance of the tomb'.

Scripture teaches us that 'it is appointed for man to die once' (Hebrews 9:27). There await us the coffin, the funeral, the worms and the corruption. One thing, however, should comfort believers, and that is the thought that the grave is the place where Jesus once lay. As surely as he rose again victorious from the tomb, so surely shall all who believe in him rise gloriously in the day of his appearing. Jesus himself was once in the grave on our behalf, and he has robbed death of its sting. 'Death is swallowed up in victory ... But thanks be to God, who gives us the victory through our Lord Jesus Christ' (1 Corinthians 15:54,57).

The great matter that concerns us all, is to make sure that we are spiritually buried with Christ, while we are yet alive, being joined to him by faith, having died to sin, and being conformed to his image.

Chapter 16

16:1–8

Let us observe, in this passage, *the power of strong love to Christ.* We have a delightful illustration of this in the conduct of Mary Magdalene, Mary and Salome, who 'bought spices, so that they might go and anoint' Jesus. 'And very early on the first day of the week, when the sun had risen, they went to the tomb.'

To visit the grave in the dim twilight of an eastern daybreak will itself have required courage. But to visit the grave of one who had been put to death as a common criminal, and to arise early to show honour to one whom their nation had despised—this was indeed a mighty boldness. Yet these are the kind of acts which show the difference between weak faith and strong faith—between weak feeling and strong feeling towards Christ. These godly women had tasted of our Lord's pardoning mercies. Their hearts were full of gratitude to him for light, hope, comfort and peace. They were willing to risk all consequences in testifying to their affection for their Saviour. 'Many waters cannot quench love, neither can floods drown it' (Song of Songs 8:7).

Why do we not see more of this strong love to Jesus among Christians? There is only one answer. A low and feeble sense of sin will always produce a low and feeble sense of the value of salvation. A slight sense of our debt to God will always be attended by a slight sense of what we owe for our redemption. It is the one who feels much forgiven who loves much. 'But he who is forgiven little, loves little' (Luke 7:47).

Let us observe, secondly, *how the difficulties which Christians fear will sometimes disappear as they approach them.* As these women walked to Jesus' grave, they were full of fears about the stone at the door. 'And they were saying to one another, "Who will roll away the stone for us from the entrance of the tomb?"' But their fears were needless. Their expected trouble was found not to exist. 'And looking up, they saw that the stone had been rolled back.'

What a striking emblem this provides of the experience of many Christians. How often believers are oppressed and cast down by anticipation of evils—and yet, in the time of need, find that the very thing they feared was removed, and the stone rolled away. A large proportion of the Christian's anxieties arise from things which never actually happen. As we look forwards to all the possibilities of the journey to heaven, we conjure up in our imagination all kinds of crosses and obstacles, and we carry tomorrow's troubles as well as today's. Yet so often we find—at the end—that our doubts and fears were groundless, and that the thing we most dreaded never happened. Let us pray for more practical faith, believing that, in the path of duty, we shall never be entirely forsaken. Let us go forward boldly, and we shall often find that the lion in the way is chained, and the seeming hedge of thorns is only a shadow.

Let us observe, thirdly, *that the friends of Christ have no cause to be afraid of angels*. 'And entering the tomb, they saw a young man sitting on the right side, dressed in a white robe, and they were alarmed.' But at once they were reassured by what he said to them: 'Do not be alarmed. You seek Jesus of Nazareth, who was crucified.'

At first sight, this lesson may seem of little importance, since we see no visions of angels in the present day. But it is a lesson which we may find useful at some future time. The day is drawing near when the Lord Jesus will come again to judge the world, with all the angels around him. On that day, these angels 'will gather his elect from the four winds, from one end of heaven to the other' (Matthew 24:31).

Let us endeavour to be known of angels as those who seek Jesus and love him in the world, and so are heirs of salvation. Let us be diligent to make our repentance sure, and so to cause joy in the presence of the angels of God. Then we shall have no cause to be afraid. We shall rise from our grave, and see in the angels our friends and fellow-servants, in whose company we shall spend a blessed eternity.

Let us observe, lastly, *the exceeding kindness of God towards his backsliding servants*. The angel's message, to be sent via the women, illustrates this. 'But go, tell his disciples and Peter that he is going before you to Galilee. There you will see him, just as he told you.' Yet notice that this message is not only directed to the apostles as a whole (though that alone, after their recent desertion of their Master, would have been amazingly gracious). Peter is singled out for individual mention—he who had sinned particularly. There were no exceptions in this deed of grace. All were to be pardoned and restored to favour—including Peter.

How easily we limit God, forgetting that 'he delights in steadfast love' (Micah 7:18). So let us leave this passage with a determination to open the door of mercy very wide to sinners, in all our making known of the gospel. And let us leave it with a resolution never to be unforgiving towards our fellow men. If Christ is so ready to forgive us, we ought to be very ready to forgive others.

[The ESV states at this point: SOME OF THE EARLIEST MANUSCRIPTS DO NOT INCLUDE 16:9–20. It provides a related footnote.]

16:9–14

Let us mark, in these verses, *what abundant proof we have that our Lord Jesus Christ really rose again from the dead.* In this passage are recorded three distinct occasions on which Jesus was seen after his resurrection: to Mary Magdalene, to two disciples 'as they were walking into the country', and 'to the eleven themselves as they were reclining at table'. Other appearances of Jesus are described elsewhere in the New Testament. So let us not hesitate to believe that, of all the facts of our Lord's history, there is none more thoroughly established than the fact that he rose from the dead.

There is great mercy in this. The resurrection of Christ is one of the foundation stones of Christianity. It was the seal of the great work which he came on earth to accomplish. It was the crowning proof that the ransom he paid on the cross for sinners was accepted, Satan was defeated, and a great victory was won. Paul declares of Jesus that he 'was delivered up for our trespasses and raised for our justification' (Romans 4:25). Peter rejoices in God that, 'According to his great mercy, he has caused us to be born again to a living hope through the resurrection of Jesus Christ from the dead' (1 Peter 1:3).

Let us mark, secondly, *our Lord Jesus Christ's special kindness to Mary Magdalene*. We are told that 'when he rose early on the first day of the week, he appeared first to Mary Magdalene, from whom he had cast out seven demons'. In doing this, Jesus meant to show how much he values love and faithfulness. Last at the cross and first at the grave, this warm-hearted disciple was allowed to be the first to see Jesus, when his victory was won. It was intended to be a permanent memorial to the church that those who honour Christ, he will honour.

Let us mark, lastly, *how much weakness there is sometimes in the faith of the best Christians*. Three times in these verses mention is made of the unbelief of the eleven apostles: when Mary Magdalene told them that Jesus was risen, when they were told by the two who had been 'walking into the country', and when Jesus himself appeared to them 'as they were reclining at table, and he rebuked them for their unbelief and hardness of heart'. These eleven men had been told repeatedly by Jesus that he would rise again; yet, when the time came, all that was forgotten, and they were found unbelieving.

Yet let us see in these men's doubts the overruling hand of an all-wise God. If those were convinced at last, who were so unbelieving at first, how strong indeed is the proof that Christ rose. The very doubts of the eleven apostles are the confirmation of our own faith. For ourselves, let us resist unbelief, watching and praying to be delivered from its power. But let us not conclude that we have no grace, because we are sometimes troubled with doubts.

Moreover, let us not fail to ask ourselves whether we have risen with Christ and been made partakers spiritually of his resurrection. This, after all, is the one thing needful. We must be raised from the death of sin, and walk in newness of life. This, and this only, is saving Christianity.

16:15–18

Notice here, firstly, *the parting commission which our Lord gives to his apostles*. He is addressing them for the last time. He marks out their work until he comes again, in words of wide and deep significance: 'Go into all the world and proclaim the gospel to the whole creation.'

Jesus would have us know that all the world needs the gospel. In every quarter of the globe mankind is the same—sinful, corrupt and alienated from God. And Jesus would have us know that the salvation of the gospel is to be offered freely to all mankind—the glad tidings that 'God so loved the world, that he gave his only Son' (John 3:16), and that 'Christ died for the ungodly' (Romans 5:6). We are not justified in making any exception in the proclamation, and have no warrant for limiting it.

Let us see here the strongest argument in favour of missionary work, both at home and abroad, and be unwearied in trying to do good to the souls of all mankind.

Notice here, secondly, *the terms which our Lord tells us should be offered to all who hear the gospel.* 'Whoever believes and is baptised will be saved, but whoever does not believe will be condemned.'

We are taught here the absolute necessity of faith in Christ for salvation. The one who 'does not believe' is the one who will be lost for evermore. Even if he has been baptised, that will make no difference. All shall profit him nothing if he lacks saving faith in Christ. Have we this faith?

We are also taught here the certainty of God's judgments on those who die unbelieving: 'whoever does not believe will be condemned'. How awful the words sound! There is an eternal hell for all who will persist in their wickedness, and who depart from this world without faith in Christ. 'If they were wise, they would understand this; they would discern their latter end!' (Deuteronomy 32:29). Let us take heed that this warning is not given to us in vain.

Notice here, lastly, *the gracious promises of special help which our Lord holds out in his parting words to his apostles.* He knew well the enormous difficulties of the work which he had just commissioned them to do. He knew the mighty battles they would have to face with heathenism, the world and the devil. And so he cheers them by telling them of certain miracles which would help forward their work.

The age of miracles is now long passed; they were never intended to continue beyond the first establishment of the church. But although the age of physical miracles is passed, we may take comfort in the thought that the church of Christ shall never lack Christ's special help in its seasons of special need. The great Head in heaven will never forsake his believing members. His eye is continually upon them, and he will always time his help wisely.

And let us never forget that Christ's believing church in the world is itself a standing miracle. The conversion and perseverance in grace of every member of that church is itself a sign and wonder. Let us thank God for this and take courage.

16:19–20

These verses tell us where our Lord went, when he left this world and ascended up on high. They tell us what his disciples experienced after their Master left them, and what all true Christians may expect until he appears again.

Mark, in these verses, *the place to which our Lord went when he had finished his work on earth, and the place where he is at the present time.* We are told that 'he was taken up into heaven and sat down at the right hand of God'. He returned to that glory which he had with the Father before he came into the world. He received, as our victorious Mediator and Redeemer, the highest position of dignity and power in heaven which our minds can conceive. There he sits—not idle, but carrying on the same blessed work for which he died on the cross. There he lives—ever making intercession for all those who come to God by him, and so 'able to save [them] to the uttermost' (Hebrews 7:25).

There is strong consolation here for all true Christians. They live in an *evil* world, and are often troubled about many things, and sorely cast down by their own weaknesses and infirmities. They live in a *dying* world, feeling their bodies gradually failing and giving way, and having before them the prospect of launching forth into a world unknown. What then shall comfort them? They must lean back on the thought of their Saviour in heaven—never slumbering or sleeping, and always ready to help. We travel on towards a dwelling where our best Friend has gone before, to 'prepare a place for (us)' (John 14:2). Jesus has entered heaven 'as a forerunner on our behalf' (Hebrews 6:20). Of him, Paul writes, 'who was raised—who is at the right hand of God, who indeed is interceding for us' (Romans 8:34).

Mark also, in these verses, *the blessing which our Lord Jesus Christ bestows on all who work faithfully for him.* 'And they went out and preached everywhere, while the Lord worked with them and confirmed the message by accompanying signs.'

We know well from the Acts of the Apostles, and from the pages of church history, the manner in which these words have been proved true, and that—in spite of every effort of Satan—the word of truth has not been preached in vain. Believers have been gathered out of the world, churches have been founded all over the world, and the little seed of Christianity has grown gradually into a great tree.

Let us not doubt that this is to be for our encouragement. No one will ever work faithfully for Christ, only to find at last that the work has been altogether without profit. Let us labour on patiently, each in our own position—preaching, teaching, speaking, writing, warning, testifying—and let us rest assured that our labour is not in vain. We ourselves may die, seeing little or no result for our work. But the last day will assuredly prove that the Lord Jesus always works with those who work for him. So let us 'be steadfast, immovable, always abounding in the work of the Lord' (1 Corinthians 15:58). We may go on our way heavily, sowing with many tears; but the divine promise is sure, that we 'shall come home with shouts of joy, bringing (our) sheaves with (us)' (Psalm 126:6).

Let us close with self-inquiry and self-examination. Let it not content us to have seen with our eyes and heard with our ears, the things written here for our learning about Jesus Christ. Let us ask ourselves whether we know anything of Christ dwelling 'in (our) hearts through faith' (Ephesians 3:17)? Does the Spirit indeed 'witness with our spirit that we are children of God' (Romans 8:16)? Can we really say that we 'live by faith in the Son of God' (Galatians 2:20)? These are solemn questions, demanding serious consideration. May we never rest until we can give them satisfactory answers! 'Whoever has the Son has life; whoever does not have the Son of God does not have life' (1 John 5:12).